Contents

Editorial 2
Caroline Sweetman

Men, masculinity, and 'gender in development' 8
Andrea Cornwall

Men, masculinities and the politics of development 14
Sarah C White

Disintegration conflicts and the restructuring of masculinity 23
Judith Large

The role of men in families: achieving gender equity and supporting children 31
Patrice L Engle

Violence, rape, and sexual coercion: everyday love in a South African township 41
Katharine Wood and Rachel Jewkes

'Crabs in a bucket': re-forming male identities in Trinidad 47
Niels Sampath

Gender workshops with men: experiences and reflections 55
Kamla Bhasin

New masculinity: a different route 62
Gonzalo Falabella G

Resources:
   Further reading 65
   Articles and papers 68
   Magazines, newsletters and journals 70
   NGOs, organisations and groups 70
   Internet resources 71

D1300043

Editorial

A focus on men, their sense of themselves as 'masculine', and the relevance of this for development, is new for most gender and development researchers and practitioners. Over the last decade, many development organisations have altered the terminology they use to discuss women's subordination from 'Women in Development' (WID) to 'Gender and Development' (GAD). This change in vocabulary reflects awareness of the fact that ideologies surrounding gender roles and identities create obstacles to women's equal economic, social, and political participation. Yet it is only relatively recently that debates on economic and social policy and 'the future of the family' have begun to bring men's gender identity, and their roles in the 'private' sphere, increasingly under scrutiny (Folbre 1994).

Men and masculinity need to be studied if power relations between the sexes are to be changed for the better, and the potential of individuals of both sexes is to be realised. Articles in this issue assess the implications for gender and development policy and practice of taking on a concern for men and concepts of 'masculinity', arguing that this is long overdue. Gisela Geisler uses words previously used by development agencies about women when she ironically suggests that 'maybe the time has come to fully and effectively "exploit the abundant potential" of men for the benefit of development' (Geisler 1993).

Focusing on women alone simply contributes to overload and exhaustion for women, if they retain all the responsibilities associated with their existing reproductive and productive roles, in an era where the state can be relied upon even less than previously to provide social services (Folbre 1994).

Ultimately, however, development organisations must decide if they are prepared to address the need to change gender relations. Continuing to work with women only — for example, targeting female-headed households as beneficiaries of funds earmarked for 'gender and development' — has allowed development organisations to side-step the uncomfortable issues associated with 'interfering' in relations between men and women within the household (Varley 1996). While it is true that female-headed households are frequently economically poorer, women living without a male partner, father or son are potentially freer to make decisions without fearing reprisals. In this sense, women living in male-headed households may well be 'poorer' than those living alone.

While development research and practice has tended to marginalise the issues of men and masculinity, researchers from other disciplines, including sociology, cultural studies and anthropology, have taken an increasing interest in studying men's gender identity and role. This work is distinguished by its focus on men's *gender* as an aspect of their identity, unlike previous work which, while centring on men, ignored gender as an aspect of social differentiation. While the rationale for studying men and masculinities varies widely (Brod and Kaufman, 1994), much of this research has been informed by a feminist perspective.

In her article, Andrea Cornwall suggests ways in which gender and development practitioners could benefit from considering such new theoretical work into gender issues.

Linking the practical to the ideological

The concept of 'hegemonic masculinity' (Connell 1987) emphasises that many variations on the concept of 'masculinity' exist within and between societies. This challenges the idea that gender identity is natural, unchanging, and 'given'. In each community, a particular form of masculinity will be widely perceived as the most desirable, and as wielding the most power — a 'hegemonic masculinity'.

Because hegemonic masculinities define successful ways of 'being a man', they make men who do not conform to that idea seem — and feel — inadequate or inferior (Cornwall and Lindisfarne 1994). A power relationship exists between men of different classes, races and abilities, in addition to the power relationship which exists between men and women (Hearn and Collinson 1994). As Sarah White highlights in her article in this issue, certain men benefit more than others since gender identity cross-cuts

other forms of social differentiation, including, race, age and economic class. While some women may benefit from their position in a patriarchal society, some men are disadvantaged.

Each man has varying 'success' in conforming to the norms of hegemonic masculinity, depending on experience, upbringing, and external context; conformity to the ideal may also come and go during the lifetime of one individual. An example of how notions of masculinity co-exist within one community is offered by Niels Sampath's article, which explores how different ideals of masculinity compete and evolve to fit changing circumstances in a Caribbean community.

The sexual division of labour is a concrete expression of ideologies surrounding gender identity. The ways in which women and men respond to changes in the sexual division of labour (including patterns of employment and income-generation) are directly connected to their sense of themselves as gendered human beings. While ideas of men's and women's work are seen in many contexts as natural and unchanging, economic and political circumstances oblige individuals to challenge or reinforce these norms continuously. As Sarah White explores in her article, the realities of who performs which tasks may belie gender ideology which labels certain activities as male or female (White, 1997). Women, as well as men, may have a vested interest in keeping up the illusion that gender ideology is being adhered to.

Men's 'triple role' as fathers

Writers in this issue and elsewhere discuss three distinct roles for men as fathers. First, men as biological fathers; secondly, as economic providers for the family; third, as what Patrice Engle, in her article, terms 'social fathers'. In common with more familiar analytical frameworks used by gender and development practitioners — for example, Caroline Moser's 'triple role' concept of women's work (Moser 1989) — these three roles emphasise that involvement in both public and private spheres is critical for family well-being.

However, the way fatherhood is experienced by individual men varies according to precedents and traditions set by wider society, current social and economic conditions, and by the dynamics of particular families and the individuals within them. While the primary role of biological fatherhood demands no commitment to the family unit which it creates, commitment from men is needed for involvement as economic providers and in 'social fatherhood'. While male fertility is a defining part of male identity cross-culturally, and the role of 'provider' is also seen as important in most societies (even while individual men may in actuality reject this responsibility), being a 'social father' — i.e. meeting the day-to-day demands of caring for children — is less commonly seen as an essential part of the male role.

Status, power and violence

A Western ideal of hegemonic masculinity has influenced the course of global development, through and beyond the colonial era, and has continued to do this through shaping the organisational culture of development institutions (Gender and Development 5:1). An emphasis on men's role as economic 'providers' comes from a polarised model of gender relations rooted in Northern industrialisation, of a male breadwinner with a wife who performs unpaid domestic work in the home, and ideals of physical strength, and solidarity between male workmates forged through struggles with managers (Connell 1993). These ideals have been exported through colonialism to mingle with local notions of masculinity:

'masculinities imported from elsewhere are conflated with local ideas to produce new configurations' (Cornwall and Lindisfarne 1994, 12).

In many industrial countries, opportunities for men to fulfil the role of sole economic provider, bringing in enough cash to support the family, are diminishing as changing global patterns of employment favour insecure, low-paid, part-time jobs for a female workforce. In the rapidly-industrialising countries in the South, a similar trend to employing women in manufacturing and the service sector is occurring. As Patrice Engle notes in her article, social policy-makers are currently addressing issues including increasing numbers of female-headed households which receive no economic support from absent fathers, and social problems including escalating male violence in the family, and rising crime among young unemployed men and boys. In their article on male violence in teenage sexual relationships in South Africa, Katharine Wood and Rachel Jewkes argue that attention should be shifted towards changing the attitudes of men; gender violence is not 'women's issue'.

In both industrialised countries and those where subsistence agriculture and small-scale income generation provide support to families, men's role in local community-based decision-making is also being eroded, through processes of 'modernisation', which have removed decision-making from community level to regional or state government bodies. In many contexts, the power of men in the community in relation to important decisions has lessened, or vanished. In Kenya, Silberschmidt claims that men have become increasingly involved in what were regarded as minor and personal decisions formerly taken by women (Silberschmidt 1991).

There is evidence that, in many situations in South and North, men's decreasing sense of political and economic power within the community is manifested in increased efforts to assert dominance within the household, marked by escalating domestic violence (Segel and Labe 1990). As a woman in a Kisii community in Kenya puts it, 'women became very busy, men took the back seat and so they began to fight' (Silberschmidt 1991, p,44).

Judith Large's article emphasises the links between different kinds of impoverishment, and violence at all levels of society. For young men in many countries, a process of alienation is resulting from the lack of economic options available to them. Large highlights the links between the socialisation of boys, lack of livelihood options for young men, and their decision to join armed groups.

Readjusting the sexual divison of labour

A frequent critique of approaches which seek to involve women in development activities is that, if these are not linked to diminishing their existing workload, the result will be simply to overburden them. While development interventions have often, therefore, sought to reduce the time and energy women expend in activities such as fuel and water collection, they have not tended to challenge the idea that domestic chores must necessarily be carried out by women and girls.

Why is it so difficult to promote the idea that men can do 'women's work'? As mentioned above, changes to either gender role are potentially threatening to both women and men since they question personal identity. Not only is doing 'women's work' unacceptable to many men, but women themselves may be unwilling to allow part of 'their role' to be taken over by their partner (Engle and Leonard 1995).

Will gender roles eventually change in the home as they are changing outside?

One compelling view is that changes in gender roles in the private sphere will only occur when domestic work and childcare cease to be seen as low-status occupations (Willott and Griffin 1996). From a livelihoods perspective, it can, indeed, be seen as a rational decision for an individual man — or couple — to opt to conform to the norms that a man does not take part in 'women's work'. The fact that men's and women's status is not equal in patriarchal societies means that there are different costs involved in challenging the sexual division of labour. While women who perform 'men's work' may eventually be admired, a man is more likely to lose status if he attempts to move across the dividing line. For example, a man who cooked might risk not only ridicule, but might be banned from participating in community decision-making (personal communication, Ethiopia). The question is how the necessary shift in attitude to domestic work can take place, given the iterative nature of the link between valuing the work, and the value placed on the gender of the person who performs it.

Men's attitudes to fertility

Men's role within the 'private' sphere has attracted particular attention from organisations working on sexual health and reproductive rights. A typical view is that 'men should not only share the benefits but also the hardships of birth control, that is, they must assume their rightful share of contraceptive responsibility' (Chikamata 1996,9).

However, the nature of the current interest in men as a key to achieving changes in sexual behaviour is being questioned by feminists. The typical language used is of 'involving men' (IPPF 1996). Yet men are already 'involved' in these issues, as medical practitioners, as manufacturers and suppliers of contraceptives, and as sexual partners who give a negative answer to women's request to use contraception. Organisations who are seeking to involve men are all too often seeking only to change the response of male partners to 'yes' regarding contraception and disease prevention.

Critically, 'if little or no attention is paid to the general picture — including both sexes rather than focusing the spotlight just on the men — there is the potential for family planning programmes to reinforce the status quo in gender inequalities' (Helzner 1996, 5). Secondly, in focusing on men alone, the valuable understanding of the problem which is gained by looking at the relationship between women and men is lost (ibid).

Related to this point is the fact that studying and working on male gender identity has significant resource implications for policy-makers in development. '[We] must carefully scrutinise where the financial support and personnel are coming from when men's services are established, and not rob potential or existing provision from other service users' (Pringle 1995, 167). There is a danger that 'the concept [of masculinity] may divert attention from women and gendered power relations' (Hearn 1996). Development policy-makers need to be clear on their reasons for focusing on men and male gender issues, ensuring that this work is seen as additional work on gender issues which does not divert resources away from addressing the interests of women.

Finally, advocates of human rights could legitimately question the way men are being co-opted into health debates, as 'instruments' to deliver a development goal. This uncomfortably echoes the way in which women have been used as instruments for delivering population control in the past. Ultimately, both men's and women's rights to determine their own lives are compromised by this.

Harnessing men's potential

Changes in the external environment cause men's and women's sense of self, and the relationships between them, to shift and potentially fragment. While this process can result in crisis for individual women and men, and their communities, it can also lead to positive change. But how far can men 'cease to mourn the loss of power and welcome the social benefits and personal pleasures of changing?' (Mac An Ghail 1996, 5) In her article on running gender training workshops with men, Kamla Bhasin points out that it is not immediately obvious how men's interests can be served by 'changing the system'.

This pessimism is shared by many different people — from media commentators to development workers — who commonly respond to changing patterns of male and female employment, and rising numbers of female-headed households, by condemning men for failing in their socially-ascribed role of 'provider'. Men tend to be characterised as feckless, irresponsible, and ultimately incapable of change, as Sarah White observes in her article in this issue: '"good girl/bad boy" stereotypes present women as resourceful and caring mothers, with men as relatively autonomous individualists, putting their own desires for drink or cigarettes before the family's needs'.

However, in common with all such stereotypes, this one conceals a complex situation in which men are the victims as well as women and children. When one's ideas of what it is 'to be a man' (or woman) cease to fit the external world in which one operates, alienation or an 'identity crisis' is likely to result (Silberschmidt 1991, 20). Writing stemming from the 'men's movement' frequently emphasises what men have 'lost' over the course of history, and what can be gained by admitting this and redefining masculinity (Bly 1991). In his article, Gonzalo Falabella

G. discusses the efforts of a group of Chilean men to overcome the culture of machismo and define the 'Chilean new man'. In his view, it is not difficult to see what men have to gain from challenging restrictive gender stereotypes, which hamper both women and men from exploring their full potential, and the male-dominated systems which have defined human development to date.

References

Bly R (1991) *Iron John: a book about men* Element Books:London

Brod, H and Kaufman, M (1994) *Theorising masculinities*, Sage: London.

Chikamata D (1996) 'Male needs and responsibilities in family planning and reproductive health' in *Planned Parenthood Challenges* 1996:2, International Planned Parenthood Federation: London

Cornwall A and Lindisfarne N (1994) 'Dislocating masculinity: gender, power and anthropology' in Cornwall A and Lindisfarne N (eds) *Dislocating masculinities: comparative ethnographies*, Routledge:London

Davies M (ed) (1994) *Women and violence,* Zed Books:London

Engle P and Leonard A, (1995) 'Fathers as parenting partners' in *Families in Focus: new perspectives on mothers, fathers and children*, ed Bruce J, Lloyd CB, Leonard A, Population Council, New York

Folbre N, (1994) *Who pays for the kids? Gender and the Structures of Constraint,* Routledge: London.

Geisler G (1993) 'Silences speak louder than claims: gender, household and agricultural development in Southern Africa' in *World Development* 21:12

Hearn J 1996, 'A critique of the concept of masculinity/masculinities' in Mac An Ghaill M (1996) *Understanding masculinities* Open University Press

Hearn J and Collinson D (1994) 'Theorising unities and differences between men and between masculinities' in Brod H and Kaufman M (eds) *Theorising Masculinities,* Sage:Los Angeles

Helzner J (1996) 'Gender equality remains the objective' in *Planned Parenthood Challenges* 1996:2, International Planned Parenthood Federation:London

IPPF (1996) 'A new look at male involvement' Briefing Paper, 4 November 1996, IPPF:London

Mac An Ghaill M (1996) *Understanding masculinities* Open University Press

Moser, C N (1989) 'Gender planning in the Third World: meeting practical and strategic gender needs', *World Development* 17:11.

Phillips A (1993) *The trouble with boys: parenting the men of the future* Pandora:UK

Pringle K (1995) *Men, masculinities and social welfare,* UCL Press

Segel, T and Labe, D (1990) 'Family violence: wife abuse' in McKendrick, B and Hoffman, W (eds) *People and Violence in South Africa*, Oxford University Press.

Shire C, (1994) 'Men don't go to the moon: language, space and masculinities' in Cornwall A and Lindisfarne N (eds) *Dislocating masculinity,* Routledge:London

Silberschmidt, M (1991) *Rethinking men and Gender Relations, CDR Research Report 16,* CDR: Copenhagen.

Willott S and Griffin C, 'Men, masculinity and the challenge of long-term unemployment' in Mac An Ghaill M (1996) *Understanding masculinities* Open University Press

Men, masculinity and 'gender in development'

Andrea Cornwall

This article focuses on the implications of recent work in feminist theory, and on questions of masculinity, stressing the need to take account of the complex and variable nature of gender identities, and to work with men on exploring the constraints of dominant models of masculinity.

Articles and training materials addressing 'gender issues' invariably talk about women. As Gender and Development (GAD) initiatives are specifically aimed at challenging and correcting the effects of gender inequality, this may seem hardly surprising. After all, the primary purpose is to work towards the involvement of women as equal partners in the development process. But the dilemmas faced by some of the 'other' gender, dilemmas that may equally be regarded as 'gender issues', are rarely given consideration. And gender training, one of the principal strategies of GAD practice, rarely speaks to men's experiences as men.

By disregarding the complexities of male experience, by characterising men as 'the problem', and by continuing to focus on women-in-general as 'the oppressed', development initiatives that aim to be 'gender-aware' can fail to address effectively the issues of equity and empowerment that are crucial in bringing about positive change. To make gender 'everybody's issue', strategies are required that take account of the complexities of

difference, and which return to the basic premises on which GAD is founded: that gender relations are fundamentally power relations.

Gender and Development: time to move on?

The failure of many Women In Development (WID) projects led to the realisation that targeting women alone was not enough (Kabeer 1995). Drawing on the work of feminist academics in the 1970s, and on the distinction between sex and gender that came to influence much feminist work in the 1970s and 1980s, feminist development practitioners borrowed the concept of gender as a social construct. Feminist anthropologists demonstrated that taken-for-granted assumptions about women and men reflect the ways in which culturally-specific ideas about women and men had become 'naturalised' (see, for example, Ortner 1974, Rosaldo 1974). Feminist anthropologists contended that there was nothing 'natural' about the gender inequalities that take different forms in different cultures (see, for example, MacCormack and Strathern 1980, Moore 1988).

In development, 'gender' came to refer to the socially constructed relations between women and men. The concept of GAD offered a new approach to including women in the development process; gender training became a 'means by which feminist advocates and practitioners... [sought] to de-institutionalise male privilege within development policy and planning' (Kabeer 1995:264). 'Gender analysis' offered tools for investigating the material bases of difference between women and men. Yet, gender analysis tells us very little about how gender identities and roles are experienced by individual women and men within communities. Rather, it is used to delineate distinctions between what women-in-general and men-in-general do, in order to guide planners. Sexual difference is taken as the starting point for analysis, and gross commonalities among women and men are presumed. This crude and simplistic form of analysis offers little in the way of understanding the dynamics of difference in communities. It tells us nothing of relationships among women and among men, nor of the intersection of gender with other differences such as age, status and wealth.

Bringing new thinking into development practice

While feminist theory has moved on and become more sophisticated, the impact of new thinking on development practice has been limited. Tracking the ideas that have influenced GAD back to academia offers some insights into the shortcomings of current practice.

By the early 1980s, there was considerable unease in feminist circles about the ways in which 'women' were being constructed in feminist writing. It became apparent that by focusing on Universal Woman, the mainstream feminism was disregarding differences between women: black, non-Western, working-class and lesbian women had their own struggles and faced other prejudices (see, for example, Moraga and Anzaldua, 1981). Western feminism and its category 'woman' was of relevance only to particular kinds of women and, some writers argued, failed to take account of the context of women's situations (see, for example, Mohanty, 1987).

On the other hand, if one could no longer talk of universals such as 'male dominance' or 'women's oppression', and if it was philosophically unsound to continue to assert broad-ranging theories about women's experience, then it seemed that there was little space left for feminist politics. While in the early 1980s, some feminist writers had began to question the sex/gender distinction that had become so fashionable (see, for example, Gatens 1983), by now, debates about the usefulness of a category 'woman' and the concept of 'gender' for activism raised further thorny questions (see, for example, Scott 1989).

Useful new concepts

The gulf between the academic world and those working in applied or activist fields has widened as complex theoretical language and concepts have come to dominate feminist writing. Dressed up in complicated terms and swathed in obscure language, much theoretical work on gender has become almost completely inaccessible to a casual outsider. In essence, however, a lot of recent gender theory seems like common sense. We all know from our own experience that how we feel or behave as women or men is influenced by the many different messages we receive from others about what is acceptable or appropriate; that over our lives, being a woman or man has different dimensions and that in different settings we might behave quite differently, depending on whom we interact with.

New theoretical tools have given social scientists the capacity to explore in greater detail the processes through which gender is locally constructed and the interactions in which gender makes a difference. **Discourse analysis**, for example, has been extremely useful in understanding the ways in which women and men come to adopt particular practices; work that shows a number of different, sometimes contradictory, discourses about gender offer the means to analyse how it is that people take up particular ways of seeing themselves and relating to others.[1] **Deconstruction** — the principle of taking apart taken-for-granted assumptions to explore the contradictions on which they are based — is equally valuable. Deconstructing the category 'woman' or 'man' reveals a host of assumptions, ideas and judgements, that can be understood in terms of people's experience and their cultural context.

Gender as a performance

Analysis of the ways in which gender affects particular interactions, looking at **Gender as a Performance** (Butler 1990) or in terms of the ways people make others feel 'different' from them (Kessler and McKenna 1978), offers new ways of exploring the contexts in which gender makes a difference.

Each day of our lives and over the course of our lives, the identities we have as women or men are not fixed or absolute, but multiple and shifting (Cornwall and Lindisfarne 1994). Gender relations are context-bound: in one setting we might behave in one way, while in others we might behave differently. Thinking in terms of what Hollway calls 'subject-positions' allows us to consider how people's behaviour relates to the specific contexts in which people interact. At home, at work, in the church or mosque or temple, at same-sex or family gatherings the ways in which a woman or man interacts with others may be very different. And the ways in which people are thought of as men or women also vary with the context: consider, for example, the contrast between the different masculinities and femininities in the 'subject-positions' of power-dressed career woman, loving mother, or devoted wife; or between doting father, beer-drinking lad, and dutiful son.

When we analyse our own lives, we can see just how complex and contradictory ways of thinking about gender can be. None of us live every moment of our lives in a state of subordination to others. And the relationships we have with people around us may be 'gender relations' in the sense that these are relationships in which gender makes a difference (see Peters 1995), but are in no sense merely one-dimensional power relations. As women, we may have sons, fathers, brothers, male friends or male employees in our lives with whom we have quite different kinds of relationships than those with a male lover, husband or boss. It is, in many ways, quite obvious that sweeping generalisations about gender make little sense of our own realities.

Missing masculinity? Men in gender and development

One of the most obvious gaps in gender and development studies, where new tools and new approaches are needed, is in relation to men. Old-style feminist theory dealt with them at one stroke: men were classed as the problem, those who stood in the way of positive change. And while feminist activism stressed change in attitudes and behaviour on the part of women in coming forward to claim their rights, it offered little more to men than a series of negative images of masculinity. Only by abandoning those attributes which are culturally valued as those associated with masculinity could men reprieve themselves. It is hardly any wonder that many men found this difficult. Not only were they told that they should give up positions that put them at an advantage, they were left without anything to value about being men.

Writings on men and on questions of masculinity are relatively recent, reflecting a belated recognition that men also have gender identities. Over the last decade, however, a great deal has been written on and by men. Some of this work could be seen as rather self-seeking, and lacks the critical edge evident in feminist work. There are, however, a number of excellent contributions to this field that have much to offer practitioners, such as Connell's (1987, 1995) work. In an influential early article, Carrigan, Connell and Lee (1985) outlined a theory of masculinity that drew on some of this recent thinking to argue that although there are many ways of being a man, some are valued more than others and men experience social pressure to conform to dominant ideas about being a man. They termed this 'hegemonic masculinity'. Not all men conform to the 'hegemonic' version; those who do not may find themselves disadvantaged, and even discriminated against.

Where the concept of 'hegemonic masculinity' is most valuable is in showing that it is not men per se, but certain ways of being and behaving, that are associated with dominance and power. In each cultural context, the ways in which masculinity is associated with power varies (Cornwall and Lindisfarne 1994). Some ways of being a man are valued more than others. But this is not to say that all men behave in this way. Attributes that are associated with masculinity are not always associated with men: women too can possess some of these attributes. Not all men, then, have power; and not all of those who have power are men.

In each cultural context there is a range of available models of masculinity or femininity. Not all men benefit from and subscribe to dominant values. 'Hegemonic masculinity' can be just as oppressive for those men who refuse, or fail, to conform. Yet, these men are often implicitly excluded from being part of processes of changing and confronting gender inequality because they are male.

Gender and Development work currently offers little scope for men's involvement. Resistance to messages about what may be interpreted as 'women's issues' makes more sense if the failure to adequately analyse and address men's experiences and gender identities is taken into account. Without an approach to difference that moves beyond static generalisations and works with and from personal experience to open up spaces for change, men will continue to be left on the sidelines and remain 'the problem'.

Implications for practice

So how can these theoretical tools be useful to practitioners dealing with the concrete everyday problems of development work? Firstly, they offer ways to build greater awareness of the challenges that men may face in coming to terms with changing identities and practices. If certain ways of being a man are culturally valued, then asking men to abandon these identities altogether without having anything of value to hold on to is clearly unreasonable. But if men become aware that in their own everyday lives they are already behaving differently in different settings without losing a sense of their own identities, then it may be easier to recognise some of the implications of 'hegemonic masculinity' without feeling attacked or threatened.

Secondly, by demonstrating that many men do not actually match up to idealised forms of masculinity, spaces can be opened up for reflection about how men can be disempowered or marginalised. Rather than tarring all men with the same

12

brush, looking at dimensions of difference can offer ways in which men can begin to re-evaluate some of the difficulties they face as men, and enhance awareness of situations in which the roles are reversed. By recognising that men can also feel powerless, scope can be offered for men to reflect on their behaviour towards those they feel they have power over. As behaviour is learnt, it can also be unlearnt and relearnt.

Lastly, if empowerment means enabling people to expand their 'power within' in order to have power to make their own choices, then this can equally be applied in work with men. It is often easier to resist change and remain cushioned by the comfort of familiarity. Behaving differently can raise all kinds of anxieties and threats, especially when identities might be compromised. By deconstructing cultural assumptions about being a man, awareness can be raised about the ways in which some of these assumptions leave people in a no-win situation. And by working from this analysis to build the confidence to choose to behave differently, men can be offered the means to empower themselves to change. Men who have already begun to embrace change are allies, rather than part of 'the enemy', and opportunities should be made to involve them more in Gender and Development work.

If gender is to be everybody's issue, then we need to find constructive ways of working with men as well as with women to build the confidence to do things differently. Just because some men occupy subject-positions in some settings that lend them power over people, it does not necessarily mean that these positions are congruent with all aspects of their lives and therefore define them as people.

Relatively simple tools, drawn from applications of theoretical models, and the practical tools of approaches such as Assertiveness Training, can be used to raise awareness of contradictions and of the knock-on effects of resisting change.

By working with men as human beings, rather than constructing them as 'the problem', addressing personal change can have a wider impact on the institutional changes that are needed for greater equity.

It is time to move beyond the old fixed ideas about gender roles and about universal male domination. Time to find ways of thinking about and analysing gender that make sense of the complexities of people's lived realities. Gender and development currently lacks sophisticated tools for understanding difference: is it not time that we turned our attention to creating them? Taking complexity seriously does not mean that we need to abandon completely fundamental feminist concerns with women's rights. The shattering of the old grand theories can be liberating, rather than robbing us of a place from which to speak about inequality. We have the choice to use arguments as strategies, without swallowing them whole to mask the real contradictions they raise in terms of our own lives (see Fraser 1995). Where we do need to be careful is in confusing strategic arguments about women or men-in-general with the everyday experiences of real women and men.

Andrea Cornwall works at the Centre for Development Communications, King Alfred's College, Winchester, UK
Tel / fax: (0044) 1273672306

Acknowledgements

This article draws in places on previous work developed with Nancy Lindisfarne and on discussions with Garrett Pratt. I am grateful for the insights I gained from sharing ideas with them.

Notes

1. One of the most accessible examples of this is Wendy Hollway's (1984) analysis

of gender identities and relations between young women and men.

References

Butler, J (1990) *Gender Trouble: Feminism and the Subversion of Identity*, London: Routledge.

Carrigan, T, Connell, R and Lee, J (1985) 'Towards a new sociology of masculinity', *Theory and Society* 14:5. .

Cornwall, A and Lindisfarne. N (1994) 'Dislocating Masculinity: Gender, Power and Anthropology', in Cornwall and Lindisfarne (eds) *Dislocating Masculinities: Comparative Ethnographies*, Routledge, London.

Fraser, N (1995) 'Pragmatism, feminism and the linguistic turn' in Benhabib, S, Butler, J, Cornell, D and Fraser, N, *Feminist Contentions: A Philosophical Exchange*, London: Routledge.

Fraser, N and Nicholson, L (1988) 'Social criticism without philosophy: an encounter between feminism and postmodernism', *Theory, Culture and Society* 5.

Gatens, M (1983) 'A critique of the sex /gender distinction' in Allen, J and Patton, P (eds) *Beyond Marx? Interventions after Marx*, Sydney: Intervention.

Hollway, W (1984) 'Gender difference and the production of subjectivity' in Henriques, J, Hollway, W, Urwin, C, Venn, C and Walkerdine, V (eds) *Changing the Subject: Psychology, Social Regulation and Subjectivity*, London: Methuen.

Kabeer, N (1995) *Reversed Realities: Gender Hierarchies in Development Thought*. London, Verso.

Kessler, SJ and McKenna, W (1978) *Gender: An Ethnomethodological Approach*, New York, Wiley.

MacCormack, C and Strathern, M (eds) (1980) *Nature, Culture and Gender*, Cambridge: Cambridge University Press.

Mohanty, C T (1987) 'Under Western eyes: feminist scholarship and colonial discourses', *Feminist Review*, 30:61-88.

Moore, H (1988) *Feminism and Anthropology*, Polity Press, London.

Moraga, C and Anzaldua, G (1981) *This Bridge Called My Back: Writings By Radical Women of Color*, Persephone, Watertown, Mass.

Ortner, S (1974) 'Is female to male as nature is to culture?' in Rosaldo, M Z and Lamphere, L (eds) *Women, Culture and Society*, Stanford: Stanford University Press.

Peters, P (1995) 'Uses and abuses of the concept of "female headed households" in research on agrarian transformation and policy', in Bryceson, D F (ed) *Women Wielding the Hoe: Lessons from Rural Africa for Feminist Theory and Development Practice*, Oxford:Berg.

Rosaldo, M Z (1974) 'Women, culture and society: a theoretical overview' in Rosaldo and Lamphere (op. cit.).

Scott, J W (1989) 'Gender: a useful category of historical analysis' in Weed, E (ed) *Coming To Terms: Feminism, Theory, Politics*, London: Routledge.

Men, masculinities, and the politics of development

Sarah C White

Widening the gender perspective to include men and masculinities should broaden and deepen our understanding of power and inequality, not only between men and women but in other social relationships, and thus increase the effectiveness of development interventions.

*A*n NGO in the Philippines was doing a study of household budgeting. Raul, a male group member, was asked about his household's finances. The income came to only half of the expenditure. Cautiously, the NGO worker suggested that perhaps his wife Anna also earned some income. Raul was enraged: he was the man of the house, he was the sole provider. He was the only one with capital — water buffaloes and coconut palms — with which to support the family. Anna, sitting nearby, signalled to the NGO worker to let it go. A few days later, the worker returned. This time Raul was absent. Anna spoke to him. She had been thinking about how the family managed. Up to then, she also had believed that her husband provided most of the family income. But when they had done the accounts, she had seen it was not so.

Each morning, Anna said, she took on credit 1 kilo of flour and some sugar from the co-operative store. She made some cheap bread, shakoys, and took it to the school gates to sell. In the evening she returned the flour and sugar to the store, and kept the income for housekeeping. Twice a week, on market days, she took two kilos of flour, and sold the shakoys *in the market place. She had no capital, so had not thought of the income as significant. Now she realised that in fact it came to as much as her husband provided. None of the income from the coconut wine came to the housekeeping anyway, he kept that for his own gambling and cigarettes.*
(White, 1994:103-4)

Examples like this are common in the Gender and Development (GAD) literature. They are usually used to show the significance of the 'invisible' contributions of women to family livelihoods. But they can also be read in another way. Certainly the story tells us something about women. But it also, very importantly, tells us something about men. Raul's sense of himself *as a man* required that he be the main provider for the family. This was also the role prescribed for him by his society. The sensitivity of this issue is shown in his anger at the mere suggestion that his wife might also be earning. Anna signalled the worker to be quiet and chose to speak only in her husband's absence because she knew how central the idea of himself as the 'breadwinner' was to his self-esteem. Peace at home and the family's status in the community depended on this. Even when Anna saw that her income was just as important as her husband's, she chose not to confront him.

Gender identity is clearly as much an issue for men as it is for women. This is just beginning to be recognised in development practice, with men's groups organised to discuss fatherhood or tackle issues of alcoholism or violence in the home. These are, however, very marginal initiatives. Mainstream development takes men's gender identities for granted, and even the move from 'Women in Development' (WID) to 'Gender and Development' (GAD) did little to shake the overwhelming preoccupation with women. Despite this, men throughout the world are behaving in ways that conform to their sense of what it is to 'be a man' in their context; and women throughout the world are manoeuvring within or contesting this. In this paper I argue that agencies and analysts should take seriously how this everyday practice affects development outcomes, and suggest some of the challenges that this involves for our existing approaches to work on gender issues.

Gender as relationship

The example of Raul and Anna makes it very clear that gender identities affect relationships. For Anna's contribution to the family livelihood to be recognised openly, Raul would need to accept a more flexible model of male/female identities. His refusal to do this meant that she had to work a 'double day', taking on part of 'his' responsibility for earning as well as all the child-care and domestic work. This is just one example of a much more general rule. Change in gender relations cannot take place in a vacuum. This is the foundation for believing that men and masculinities must be made an issue in gender planning:

if positive changes are to be achieved for women, men must change too.[1]

This does not, of course, necessarily mean that issues of masculinity need to be tackled directly. Perhaps the most sustainable kind of change comes from the 'bottom up', as men are confronted by their women's new assertiveness. A challenge from Anna would force Raul to respond either defensively with anger, violence or withdrawal; or by welcoming the change in their relationship and re-working his sense of himself as a man within that. The difficulty is that gender does not belong only to the particular relationship between husband and wife, but to much broader patterns of relationship between men and men, and between women and women. If Raul decided to give up cigarettes and gambling, he might well face ridicule from his male smoking and betting partners. Anna might find support from her friends, but she might also find that they, or other women in the family, counsel her to keep quiet, calling on ideals of feminine submission. If Raul's male peers were already questioning the conventions together it would be much easier for him to change. Similarly, a male culture which condemns violence and values flexibility makes a positive response to women's challenge much more likely.

The logic of this is clear. If women alone work for greater equality in gender relations they will face an uphill struggle. It will be another kind of 'double day', where they have to take responsibility not only for changing their own ideologies and practice, but those of their men as well. Changing oneself is hard enough; trying to change someone else often seems doomed to failure. Coupled with this, the intimacy, complexity, and entrenched character of gender relations mean that a sustained campaign, following multiple lines of attack, is called for. Women may need to be the prime movers. But their task will be impossible unless a dynamic is generated amongst men to question their personal practice and the ideologies of masculinity which it embodies.

Men's private stories

A theme in work on gender is the need to counter the 'public' orthodoxy by listening to 'private' stories. In the example given above, the public orthodoxy 'men are the breadwinners' was corrected by Anna's private account of her earnings. But to focus only on women leaves intact the 'public story' for men, and so perpetuates a series of biases.

In the gender and development literature men appear very little, often as hazy background figures. 'Good girl/bad boy' stereotypes present women as resourceful and caring mothers, with men as relatively autonomous individualists, putting their own desires for drink or cigarettes before the family's needs.[2] The overtones in this of colonial stereotypes about 'lazy natives' are uncomfortable, to say the least. Recognition of women's involvement in the market needs to be complemented by an acknowledgement of the part men play in the family. Emphasis on the opposition between women and men needs to be balanced with investigation of the conflicts and contradictions within and between men. A first step in analysing men and masculinities, therefore, is to explore the 'private stories' of men, and how they support or contradict the public ideologies of masculinity.

Studies of boys growing up suggest a considerable struggle to establish an opposition between masculine and feminine out of an earlier experience of gender identity as more ambivalent and continuous. Unlike the imagery of established patriarchal power, most studies show masculinity as rather fragile, provisional, something to be won and then defended, something under constant threat of loss. As Gilmore (1990:11) reverentially states, real manhood is 'a precarious or artificial state that boys must win against powerful odds'.

From a different standpoint, Deniz Kandiyoti (1994) considers the tensions boys may experience growing up in a purdah society. She suggests that the strict division between male and female spheres sets up a sharp contradiction for boys, who spend their first years in almost wholly female company and then have to make 'an abrupt and possibly disturbing entry into the male world' (*ibid*:204). She quotes Khan's (1972) observations on the contradictions of purdah in boys' development, where the father appears as authoritarian patriarch leading a fearful or resentful son to side with his mother. Something similar is suggested for Indian society by psycho-analyst Sudhir Kakar (1981). The close identification of sons with their mothers in the first five years is abruptly severed as they enter the male world. This 'second birth' is marked by new, and increasingly stringent, discipline. Unconditional mother love is replaced by conditional approval from men in the family. Kakar sums up this process by quoting a North Indian proverb: '"Treat a son like a *raja* for the first five years, like a slave for the next ten and like a friend thereafter."' (Kakar, 1981:127).

Both authors see this childhood experience as having life-long effects, with Kandiyoti in particular believing that it sows the seeds of later 'pro-feminist' sympathies in men. Certainly there is much more affection, support and solidarity across gender lines than much of the literature suggests. Regarding South Asia, for example, great stress is laid on son preference and the economic disaster of having too many daughters in the context of high dowry demands. A small incident demonstrated to me how partial this is. I was sitting with the father of the family with whom I stayed during my research in Bangladesh, and some of his male friends. Another neighbour joined us, close to tears. He explained that he had

had to leave his own home, as they were preparing for his daughter's wedding and he couldn't bear to lose her. The sympathy with which the other men received him showed that this was a common feeling they all shared. Nor was this an isolated incident. It was reinforced by the consistently easy and affectionate relationship which my host enjoyed with his six-year-old daughter, which allowed her even to criticise his behaviour within a framework of jokes and teasing.

As noted above, the ideology of male autonomy is a powerful one. Gilmore (1990:223) expresses this in glowing terms:

Manhood is a kind of male procreation: its heroic quality lies in its self-direction and discipline, its absolute self-reliance — in a word in its agential autonomy.

Attending to men's family relationships offers a corrective to this. Countering the tendency she sees to concentrate on solidarity between women, Fonseca (1991) notes that amongst slum-dwellers in Brazil, brothers were the most important sources of external support to women. Where households and families are much more stable, as in Bangladesh, the family is a formidable institution of social control. The relations involved, of course, differ according to gender and birth placing, but the fact of very distinct and demanding expectations is constant. The interrelation of power and responsibility is very evident. An eldest son, for example, has considerable authority over his siblings, but it would be hard to argue that he enjoys autonomy. On the contrary, the demands on him to assume family leadership are often experienced in considerable tensions between the interests of his natal family and conjugal unit. Men may have more room for manoeuvre than women, but the difference is a question of degree.

A further check on the claims of male autonomy lies in the association of masculinities with status. To some extent this is an issue between men and women. Hetero-

sexual performance, for example, appears as a significant area of male anxiety. Nick Hornby's novel *High Fidelity* is testament to this in contemporary Britain; Gilmore (1990:74) echoes it for Trukese society as he quotes Thomas Gladwin's (1953) comment that intercourse is a contest in which only men can lose.[3] But the broader context within which men negotiate their relationships with women is their standing in society *with respect to other men.* Tales of sexual exploits are thus common currency in male-male discussions, while conversely, women's unlicensed sexual expression is a threat to male prestige.

That relations between men and women rest on broader patterns of competition between men is illustrated by Penelope Harvey (1994:76) in an example from the Peruvian Highlands. There, she says, women may use courts against men guilty of infidelity, but a man would never do the same, as to admit publicly that his woman had been unfaithful would be to undermine his authority before the male hierarchical figure of the judge. Manhood certainly does not appear to be self-reliant and autonomous. On the contrary, masculinity seems to depend chronically on the estimation of others, to be highly vulnerable to attack by ridicule, shaming, subordination, or 'dishonourable' female action.

The stress on male status makes masculinity largely a matter of public performance. But the sense of oneself as a man has also a highly intimate dimension. For a man I knew in Bangladesh, his whole sense of self began to crumble when he discovered his wife was having an affair. Theirs had been a love marriage, and in the early years, he said, he considered himself the happiest man alive. His wife stopped the affair, but it then recurred, and her husband never recovered. He suffered a series of mysterious illnesses. He stopped working, stayed lying in the house in a darkened room, and avoided community events in which he used to take an active part. Deeply depressed, he was no longer able to support the family. He lost the capacity to lead, to take decisions; although the oldest brother in his own family, he allowed the others to determine even major issues. His status fell sharply, as his sons and brothers became irritated and then despising, and respect in the wider community turned to whispers of scandal and then exclusion. While not conforming to dominant gender models, this 'deviant' behaviour still makes implicit reference to them (see Abu Lughod, 1986). In a sense he became feminised, as he withdrew from the outside world. But his decline also had a clear masculine script: he punished himself and his family through serious alcohol abuse.[4]

Counting the cost

The costs to men of models of masculinity can be seen at the public level too. Perhaps the crudest indicator in any 'quality of life' index is the capacity to survive. The over-whelming recruitment of men as fighters by both state and revolutionary forces puts them in great danger. The highest rates of homicide in the United States are found amongst young black men. Men in the North have a life expectancy consist-ently several years less than that of women, suggesting the costs of gender-related occupational and consumption patterns. At a less stark level, many men suffer as they try to adjust their sense of themselves with the demands that society makes on them. Many men are unable to build good relationships with their children because they have to spend too much time away from home working. Clearly, the current constitution of gender identities causes problems for men, as well as for women.

Incorporating this into gender analysis is not straightforward. We need to go beyond saying 'poor men'; that men have problems too, that both genders are disadvantaged. To do so risks undermin-ing any project for change in gender relations, and so reinforcing existing

limitations faced by men and women. Another set of data testifies to the huge advantage of men over women with respect to access and control over material resources; religious, organisational, and political power; and rights over their own bodies and those of others. Men may suffer too, but structurally they clearly benefit from gender inequality, even those who do not conform to society's ideas of what men should be. Kandiyoti (1988) uses the term 'patriarchal bargain' to explain why women collude in gender subordination — they know that even if they suffer while young, they will be rewarded later by gaining some power over other women. Men also strike various patriarchal bargains: they lose something, but they also stand to gain much.

Gender, age, race and class

What difference will studying men and masculinities make to the frameworks we use to analyse gender in development? First, the competition between men that masculin-ity involves raises the question of whether gender may similarly generate conflicts between women. That gender does not provide an automatic basis for solidarity has long been recognised. Molyneux (1985) points out the diversity of 'women's interests': some of which derive from their gender identity, but others from factors such as race and class. She proposes the notion of 'gender interests', for those derived specifically from structural inequality by gender. Practical interests lie in bettering one's situation within the existing system (such as women having access to affordable childcare). Strategic interests relate to structural change of the system (for instance, challenging the assumption that domestic work is women's responsibility).

This framework can reveal how gender-based divisions between women may arise. Taking the example of Kandiyoti's 'patriarchal bargain', it is the practical gender interests of older women which limit most strictly the gender interests of their younger kin.

The practical and strategic dimensions of gender interests thus set up difference, and the potential for conflict, both within women and amongst them. Common oppression can become a rallying cry for collective action, but by no means always does so. Establishing contradictions of interest within the subordinate group is one way in which dominance is secured.

A second important implication of 'counting men in' is the attention it brings to status, and to the connections between gender, age, race and class. This suggests that all these interests are dynamically related, shaping and being shaped by each other in turn. Considering male gender identities brings out the extent to which the apparently neutral 'class' or 'national' interest may in fact be implicitly related to male gender stereotypes. An example may help to clarify this. The speaker is Bolai, a Bangladeshi landless labourer. At the time, 20 taka (including food) was the average daily male wage in the area.

Listen, let me tell you something. It was the lean time, and we weren't getting work anywhere. I'd come back home and my kids were crying: Dad, I'm hungry; and I had nothing to give them to eat. So we went to Fazlur and asked if he had any work. He said he had some earth work that needed doing, how much would we take? So we thought: it's the lean time, there's no point in hustling and asking a lot. If we get six Taka we can just about manage. So that's what we asked for.

So he said: O, my son's just bought a Honda, six Taka, how can I manage that! So, there we are, listening to the tale of his woes. In the end he says: I'll give you three Taka. Three Taka for a day's work! So we thought and said, Give us one Taka more, give us four. And he said: O how can I manage that? I'll give you three and a half Taka, take it or leave it, that's my last word. So we took it. What can we do? They know we have no choice.
(White, 1992:47)

The primary context of this interaction is clearly one of class relations. It provides a text-book account of the reproduction of class inequality to the advantage of the rich and the further impoverishment of the poor. But interestingly, both of the protagonists also draw on their gender identities. Bolai's position as labourer, and Fazlur's capacity as employer, are both based on their identities as men. Both of them also make reference to their (gender) role as father in mitigating their part in the interaction. Bolai frames his acceptance of the low rates of pay in terms of his responsibilities as father, perhaps thereby reclaiming some masculine honour from an otherwise shaming subordination. Fazlur legitimates his refusal to provide a living wage by reference to his own need to provide his son with a motorbike — itself a totem of masculinity in that village context. Bolai's bargaining strength is further undermined by his ethnicity — a minority Adivasi — against Fazlur's dominant status as Muslim Bengali. Class interests are thus expressed in gender-related ways, but the role that gender plays is equivocal: it at once helps structure the system of domination and is used by both actors to bargain over the terms of engagement.

Masculinity and values

Development is concerned with the practical. The great desire is to make a difference. In this context, is not talking about masculinities a retreat into the abstract, a pursuit of academic interest only? To answer this, it is important to review different aspects of gender relations. We tend to see gender in dualistic ways, with men and women as different and opposing categories. But what are considered 'masculine' or 'feminine' attributes (and these differ by social context) are found in both men and women. Ian Craib, a British psychologist and sociologist, states that in the counselling groups with which he has worked there was no simple pattern of men being aggressive or women passive, as the imagery of masculine and feminine prescribe (1994:139). What this means, is that gender is not only to do with persons, but also very importantly, with values. Connell (1995:223) brings these two dimensions together:

Masculinity is shaped in relation to an overall structure of power (the subordination of women to men), and in relation to a general symbolisation of difference (the opposition of femininity to masculinity).

As a set of values, masculinity is available to women as well as men. It was, for example, during Margaret Thatcher's time as Prime Minister in the UK that the term 'wets' was coined for those members of the Conservative Party who did not agree with her hard line. The gender critique of the policies she instituted is familiar with respect to structural adjustment (eg Elson, 1991). What is important to recognise is that these outcomes are not coincidental, but derive from the fact that the economic policies followed are inscribed in a particular model of masculinity. It is also vital to note that this 'macho' style of politics did not simply serve to advantage (some) men over (some) women, but to reproduce and intensify much broader patterns of domination by race and class as well. Different styles of masculinity are developed historically, not given for all times and places. Those now dominant are therefore integrally interwoven with 'development' — through colonialism, the movement towards modernity, and now globalisation. To explore masculinities therefore represents not only a challenge to gender analysis, but to the power and culture of the development enterprise as a whole.

Masculinity and development practice

If the argument of this paper is correct, it means that treating gender as solely a women's issue seriously underestimates the scale of the battle to achieve a more just society. This has major implications for the GAD approach, in relation to the issue of 'empowerment'.

Empowerment has usually been conceived in terms of women's growing self-confidence and ability to act ('power to') rather than women 'taking power' ('power over') from men (see eg Moser, 1989:1815). Nevertheless, it is very clear that if women's empowerment is to be sustained, it must be complemented by a change for men. The scant attention so far paid to male interests or needs has as yet resulted in relatively little fall-out, perhaps reflecting the limited success of many 'empowerment' initiatives. Nevertheless, there are danger signs. Probably the most lauded development programme world-wide is the Grameen Bank savings and credit programme for poor women in Bangladesh. While still tentative, there are reports that this programme has been associated with an increase in violence against women in the home (Goetz and Sen Gupta, 1994:19). It is possible, that the violence represents men's 'struggle for the maintenance of certain fantasies of identity and power' (Moore 1994:154) in the context of a public assault on established gender norms which has totally failed to take their interests into account. This may be too alarmist, but it is a real possibility. The 'backlash' against feminism in the United States and the establishment of neo-conservative men's groups, both black and white, provide strong arguments for taking this seriously.

Secondly, while gender-oriented programmes broadly aim to make women less poor, as well as 'more empowered', they still tend to focus on gender in isolation from other social relations. Considering masculinity, however, points up how gender also plays a part in the other relations of inequality which structure society. Changes in gender relations should thus be expected to challenge other kinds of power relations, by class, age and by race. This has two practical implications. First, that working for change on gender will meet all kinds of resistance, from men and women defending their status with respect to age, class or race, not simply gender in itself. Second, that working on gender should bring out, rather than obscure, broader issues of inequality: amongst women and amongst men, as well as between the sexes.

To take this on will mean re-orienting GAD practice from assuming gender as the endpoint to making it the entry point for further analysis. As many have pointed out, the price of 'mainstreaming' (which is still far from complete) has been a shift from seeing it as a political issue (what had posed as universal excluded the interests of half of the human race!) to a technical one, which could be incorporated within the existing model of development with only major adjustments. What has received less attention, is that the focus on gender also blocked out other considerations. Gender became *the* justice issue, women *the* 'minority' whose interests should be considered, 'social development' became, at least in some agencies, very largely commandeered by 'gender specialists'. Widening the picture to include consideration of men and masculinities should not simply 'count men in', but also broaden and deepen our understanding of power and inequality.

Ways forward

What does all this mean for development practice? Does it simply amount to a watering down of the manifesto for change in gender relations, to a weak position which states that 'men have problems too'? And even if it is accepted that men need to change, how is this to be brought about? Should we be looking to establish men's groups with a focus on gender, parallel to those which already exist for women?

R W Connell's review of the experience of men's 'consciousness-raising' groups in the West, suggests that this is not the best way forward. Men do not, like women, have a common structural interest in changing gender relations. Despite the struggles within and between them, they still benefit overall from the existing system. This means that men's groups are inherently unstable and often short-lived; they tend to retreat from the political into the personal; and can easily shift from being pro-feminist to quite hostile, as men become defensive at having to shoulder all the blame for patriarchy (*op cit*:235-6). Connell suggests, therefore, that men are more likely to change in ways that benefit women when gender relations are questioned in the context of another shared struggle. The example he gives is the green movement, which is not explicitly concerned with gender, and yet in its methods of organising and opposing the values which threaten the environment challenges men and women to question the way they operate, and to seek alternatives.

Working with men to question their behaviour is one part of the enlarged gender project. But making an issue of masculinity also reverses the strong tendency noted by Robertson (1984:305) to 'study down', to investigate marginal groups and filter this information up to those in power. Instead, he argues, it is important to analyse the powerful themselves, those who determine development strategies, and so provide material to those below to inform and strengthen their struggles. Making an issue of masculinity therefore means not only focusing on men, but on the institutions, cultures, and practices that sustain gender inequality *along with other forms of domination, such as race and class.* This will involve questioning symbolic as well as material dimensions of power. It means working on, and recognising the connections between, the personal and professional, the politics of institutions and the global system. It will involve men and women, black and white, rich and poor working separately and together to forge strategic alliances based not simply on where they have come from, but on where they want to go.

Sarah White is a lecturer in Development Studies at the University of East Anglia, UK. Tel: (0044) 1603 592327; e-mail: s.white@uea.ac.uk

Notes

1 Further examples of this point are given in an earlier paper (White, 1994).
2 This is the way, for example, that targeting women for welfare handouts or credit intervention is commonly justified.
3 This, of course, is open to debate from a woman's perspective!
4 The association of alcohol (ab)use with masculinity is, of course, a culturally specific one.

References

Abu-Lughod, L (1986) *Veiled Sentiments: Honor and Poetry in a Bedouin Society* Berkeley: University of California Press.

Connell, R W (1995) *Masculinities* Oxford: Polity Press.

Craib, I (1994) *The Importance of Disappointment* London: Routledge.

Elson, D (1991) 'Male bias in macro-economics: the case of structural adjustment' in her (ed) *Male Bias in the Development Process* Manchester: Manchester University Press.

Fonseca, C (1991) 'Spouses, siblings and sex-linked bonding: a look at kinship organization in a Brazilian slum.' in E Jelin (ed) *Family, Household and Gender Relations in Latin America* London: UNESCO/Kegan Paul.

Gilmore, D (1990) *Manhood in the Making: Cultural Concepts of Masculinity*, New Haven and London: Yale University Press.

Goetz, A-M and Sen Gupta, R (1994) 'Who takes the credit? Gender, Power, and control over loan use in rural credit programmes in Bangladesh', *Working Paper 8*, Sussex: IDS.

Harvey, P (1994) 'Domestic violence in the Peruvian Highlands', pp. 66-89 in Harvey, P and Gow, P (eds) *Sex and Violence: Issues in Representation and Experience*, London: Routledge.

Kandiyoti, D (1988) 'Bargaining with Patriarchy', *Feminist Studies* 2.

--------------- (1994) 'The paradoxes of masculinity: some thoughts on segregated societies' in Cornwall, A and Lindisfarne, N (eds) *Dislocating Masculinity: Comparative Ethnographies* London: Routledge.

Molyneux, M (1985) 'Mobilisation without emancipation? Women's interests, the state, and revolution in Nicaragua', *Feminist Studies* 11: 2, pp. 227-254.

Moore, H (1994) 'The problem of explaining violence in the social sciences' in Harvey and Gow, op. cit.

Moser, C (1989) 'Gender planning in the Third World: meeting practical and strategic gender needs', *World Development* 17: 11. pp. 1799-1825.

Robertson, A S (1984) *People and the State: An Anthropology of Planned Development* Cambridge: Cambridge University Press.

White, S (1992) Arguing with the Crocodile: Gender and Class in Bangladesh, London: Zed Books.

---------(1994) 'Making men an issue' in Macdonald, M (ed) *Gender Planning in Development Agencies: Meeting the Challenge*, Oxford, Oxfam.

Disintegration conflicts and the restructuring of masculinity

Judith Large

This paper argues that as relief and development agencies attempt to address the dynamics of organised violence and protracted conflicts which increasingly hamper or distort their work, gender analysis and policy is in need of re-examination, and should be widened to take on the issue of male gender identity.

Somali women comment on the trend in Mogadishu to name male infants 'Uzi' or 'AK' (Mohamed 1996); Chechen women hide their sons in dark cellars to avoid kidnapping or forcible conscription (Satterwhite 1996); and data on child soldiers in 24 countries reveals these to be overwhelmingly boys (Brett, 1996). UNICEF blames lightweight weapons for the 'frightening escalation' in the number of child soldiers (UNICEF 1995). As Atsango Chesoni has stated:

Peace is about transformation, and the quest for peace entails a social reconstruction of masculinity that goes beyond male chauvinism to a masculinity no longer built on subjugation. Patriarchy needs to be transformed into true brotherhood, a brotherhood that is capable of recognising women's sisterhood. (Chesoni 1995, 8)

As a creative tension or dynamic, conflict may be an inherent factor in processes of change. Yet, in the last part of the twentieth century, 'wars of liberation or state formation have been superseded by political violence linked to state disintegration and, in the context of systemic crisis, violence has become an important part of economic and political survival' (Byrne, 1995 4, citing Duffield 1994).

The complexity of conflict

The 'disintegration conflicts' discussed by Byrne (ibid.) cover a spectrum of power interests, civilian dislocation, high casualties, groupings and regroupings of armies and para-military units. Conventional definitions of war are inadequate to convey the complexities of the causes or nature of contemporary conflict; for example, El-Bushra and Piza-Lopez observe that 'international' and 'intra-state' conflicts are not necessarily mutually exclusive categories. The Gulf War, for example, was inextricably linked with other internal and regional conflicts (El-Bushra and Piza-Lopez, 1993).

It is clear that post-cold-war transitions include new extremes in disintegration, civil war and so-called 'protracted social' or 'low intensity' conflicts. A UNICEF report published in December 1995 states that 90 per cent of victims of conflict are now civilians instead of soldiers. Women and children constitute some 80 per cent of the world's refugees (Beijing Report).

Neither religion nor ethnicity provide an adequate explanation for the causes of intra-state conflict: we are witnessing in some instances the massive manipulation of populations to carry out murder in the name of a myriad of political interests. In many conflicts, the lines between political and criminal activity have become blurred; armed attacks in Sierra Leone, Liberia, Georgia, or Northern Ireland defy clear-cut or traditional explanations in terms of rebellion, armies, aims, or motives. Armed conflict seems to have become a means of transaction in the illegal diamond trade in Sierra Leone, drugs in Northern Ireland or Los Angeles, or protection rackets in Croatia.

Gender and armed conflict

War is men's business, so we are told. Indeed, a state's decision to resort to violence is seldom taken by women. Does this mean that women are not affected by armed conflicts? On the contrary, conflict takes a heavy toll on them; and it is generally they who, quietly and behind the scenes, ensure the survival of their families and even of their communities. (ICRC 1995, 4)

This quotation is typical of much of the gender and development literature on armed conflict, in its implication that men control decision-making relating to armed conflict, and that the fighting itself is an exclusively male preserve, while women are both victims of violence and offer the keys to survival and continuity in post-conflict situations.

That this picture seriously over-simplifies women's and men's roles can be seen from literature; for example, as Moghadam has pointed out:

Standard texts on nationalism, revolution, Islamization, and state formation are rich in detail on changing forms of class hierarchies, on national-international linkages, on causes of revolts, and on aspects of state capacity. But very little is explained regarding gender hierarchies, laws about women and the family, and concepts of feminine and masculine. And yet, it is becoming increasingly evident that laws and discourses pertaining to gender are central to the self-definition of political groups and, indeed, signal the political and cultural projects of movements and regimes (Moghadam 1994).

The Panos collection *Arms to Fight: Arms to Protect* (Bennet et al 1995) contains oral testimonies which document the complexities and differences in women's experiences of armed conflict, and the long-term implications of war and recovery. Women cope with the effect of the destruction of family units, nursing the disabled, caring for the orphaned, playing a central part in ensuring the survival of members of broken communities. They bear the physical and psychological consequences of rape and other forms of physical abuse which are used as weapons of war. Yet they may also be combatants, or participants in the hidden economy of armaments manufacture.

Too neat a categorisation of 'men's business' and 'women's business' in armed conflict is deeply problematic. First, the complex question of gender becomes an over-simplified one which focuses solely on gender roles, giving the impression that these are static. Denying the 'male' roles that women take on in times of crisis — for example, the combatant roles which women have taken alongside men in liberation struggles (including those in Algeria, Zimbabwe,

Vietnam, and Eritrea) — could be seen as an integral part of the processes by which women are often relegated to less-than-equal socio-economic and political roles when war is over. Similar dynamics have worked in former socialist states including Croatia and Serbia, where a constitutional commitment to women's equality under socialism has given way to a conceptualisation of women as the bearers of sons to fight for nationalist struggles (*War Report*, September 1995).

Second, attributes regarded as 'masculine' and 'feminine'[1] can be possessed by either women or men, and are not fixed either between or within societies. Women's and men's gender identities and behaviour fluctuate and change in response to external forces, including armed conflict. For example, in the Panos study, Ugandan women describe their new-found strengths and independence, but lament the loss of identity and direction experienced by their men, changes due in large part to the upheaval of war (Benner et al 1995).

Associating men with violence and women with the making of peace can legitimise violence as a natural, and therefore unquestioned, aspect of male behaviour.

Studies of national liberation struggles point out that women often become active because they see the need to defend their lovers or children — because, that is, of their gender-interests. The way that men's participation also is shaped by cultures of masculinity and gender-determined roles as fathers, husbands or lovers, sons and brothers, is not remarked (White 1993, 100).

While many feminist critiques have defined militarism as masculine, development practice has taken the concept of 'gender' and applied it with a focus only on women. That women's positions, interests and choices are influenced by their gender is recognised; the fact that men's situations are similarly affected by gender is not.

Reasons for participation in conflict

If we analyse men's experience and identity in current war and disintegration conflicts, we find a complex identity issue which undermines any simplistic assumption that violence and war-making is inherently characteristic of male human beings. The nature of involvement in armed conflict is dictated by many interlinked factors which shape particular boys and men; a hierarchy of interests and power operates within the framework of masculinity. Men may be unwilling to participate in acts of violence, yet the social relationships in which they are caught up pressurise them into complicity. *The Guardian* of 29.7.96 ran articles on both forcible conscription of young men in South Sudan and male rape in Croatia. A report from Grozny in April 1996 stated:

...the entire male population of Chechnya is subject to arbitrary detention at any time, where they are held in 'filtration camps', beaten, tortured and sometimes killed. In addition to the stated military rationale of seeing if they are 'fighters', there seems to be an economic motive for holding them as well: families can pay ransom for their freedom (personal communication).

Poverty creates an economic motive which is a factor in the complex reasons for both adults and children joining the military. While violent coercion is frequently the cause of both boy and girl children's joining in armed conflict (Frankel 1995), children may also see membership of a combative force as the only means of ensuring their survival, as the social fabric of society breaks down and traditional support systems, including their own families, cannot provide for them (Goodwin-Gill and Cohn, 1994).

Apart from receiving the material means of survival, boy soldiers may meet their need for more intangible forms of nurturing, formerly provided within the family or community, through developing a form of father-son relationship with commanding officers. This can lead to armies manipulating children's loyalty to authority figures to force them to commit atrocities: 'as fighters, these boys excelled. Their commanders served as father figures, and the children followed orders without hesitation or moral qualm' (Purvis 1995, 4, in the context of Liberia). The idea that searching for a family substitute can be a motivation for boy children joining armies has also been referred to in the context of Burma (Frankel 1995).

Conflict and contests in constructing masculinity

In the late 1970s Paul Willis published *Learning to Labour* and opened up a whole new set of questions about the construction of masculinity. Focusing on male hierarchies, Willis examined how ideas of masculinity were affected by, and themselves affect, relationships between men. In school settings, his research suggested that the definition of masculinity was not imposed from outside, but defined and contested by boys themselves. Boys subordinate other boys according to behaviour based on resistance to rules, expectations, authority of adults, and co-operative behaviour. The subordinate realm was not outside of men (women) but sought, created and separated out from within the male group (Willis, 1977).

Experiences of men in other cultures and countries confirm that such processes are a feature of male adolescence else-where. To David Gilmore (1990) who studies the ways boys became men in diverse societies, 'real manhood' is a 'precarious or artificial state that boys must win against powerful odds'.[2] Warrior images and legendary feats are ancient and universal. One example is the annual Croatian festival at Sinj. *Sinjska Alka* is a celebration of 'manly skills, spear-throwing, riding, fighting and contests of bravery' (personal communication, 1996). Over the past 300 years, this event defines *Hiduks* (front warriors) from *Ooscuts* (back warriors) and celebrates a combination of 'bravery and physical skill' (ibid.).

In many communities throughout the world, the opportunities for men to define their male identity through such physical feats are rapidly disappearing. Yet, positioning within male groupings in con-temporary society, removed from situa-tions of violent conflict, are influenced by these values in ways we do not always recognise. Similar contests appear to occur, for example, in the workplaces of modern industry, with working-class men appropriating the 'warrior' definition; while middle-class men, whose occupa-tions involve them in the acceptance of rationality and responsibility, are thrown back on the definition of masculinity as 'not female'. Generations of men who have found themselves in subordinate positions have developed the view that activities that are highly regarded and rewarded, but from which they are excluded, are 'non-masculine' (Jordan, 1995).[3]

In societies where physical strength is no longer a prerequisite for men to carry out their everyday tasks, ideals of masculine strength are promoted through cultural icons of physically forceful masculinity. The character of Rambo from American films, is widely known in countries throughout the world. In Lesotho in the late 1980s, the armed forces regularly visited the cinema to watch violent films (personal communication).

Subverting the 'warrior' discourse

Is it possible to harness the processes which socialise boys into 'warriors', in conflict and in peacetime, to capitalise on the positive aspects of male socialisation and

Cinema posters, Acre, Brazil. Cultural icons of violent masculinity exert a powerful influence.

Jenny Matthews/Oxfam

Kosovo Albanian blood feuds. Çetta, a folklorist and elder, resurrected the idea of honour in forgiving as equal to or higher than honour through 'killing in the blood' (Jani, 1995). Similarly, black township leaders in South Africa succeeded in re-directing the violence of youth gangs against each other by subordinating their rivalries to the dominant (and unifying) goal of majority rule and the end of apartheid (personal experience).

Restructuring masculinity

With narrow options to forge a livelihood and the need to achieve pride in their manhood, contemporary youth cultures in many contexts are currently recreating cycles of violence as goals in themselves. In communities at war, the lack of alternative opportunities may cause young men to volunteer, or become conscripts (Keen 1995).

This dynamic poses a profound challenge for agencies working in community relief and development. In a study comparing Uganda, Mozambique, Somalia, Liberia and Sierra Leone, Bradbury points out a number of common features — demographic change, the weakening of traditional authority structures, coupled with a global growth in youth culture and the failure of states to provide adequate educational and socio-economic opportunities. He argues that these factors have led to young men's marginalisation from society; 'the problems of youth is a strategic issue which few development agencies have begun to address' (Bradbury 1995, 11). Without alternative aspirations, sources of livelihood and fulfilment goals, the threat and use of violence is not a secondary mode of influence, but a structural underpinning of hierarchical relations. Richards describes young male terroristic violence as a proven way of making political capital, a medium of empowerment for men who have nothing else. This is not violence born of innate aggression.

Bradbury suggests that the structural factors which make armed aggression a

subvert those which are harmful to society? Ellen Jordan attempted to do this. She carried out studies in schools of rankings and behaviour in groups of boys. She found that in situations where there was violence, including bullying, it was possible to 'reclaim' those attributes of leadership and team-player/warrior behaviour which do not depend on forceful physical dominance (Jordan 1995).

A crucial part of the process, Jordan discovered, was to 'find ways of defining masculinity with the unacceptable aspects of the fighting boys' behaviour as the subordinate term, as characteristics of the weakling or the coward rather than the hero' through emphasising that modes of masculinity exist which are based on self-control and moral courage (ibid).

Another attempt to achieve a peace-making model of masculinity was made by Anton Çetta, focusing on the practice of rational way of life for young men to choose must be recognised and analysed as 'push and pull' factors (ibid.). To provide alternative options and rebuild youth confidence in their communities, and in the state, obviously requires a major investment in social development, particularly educational and employment programmes (Richards 1995). This, with informed campaigns on debt, structural adjustment and predatory corporate investment practice, is the 'macro' end of possible development response (ibid).

At the 'micro' level, concerns which are currently being addressed by development and relief organisations regarding the costs of armed conflict to men and boys include psycho-social issues: recovery from intimidation and from coercive participation in atrocities. Participation is often secured through the use of drugs, deprivation of sleep, and the compulsory viewing of violent war videos, not to mention classic 'blooding' techniques whereby young fighters are forced to kill members of their own communities or families (personal communication). For example, young demobilised soldiers in Sierra Leone have been assisted by the Children Affected by War project, supported by UNICEF and Concern Universal (presentation by Sierra Leone delegates at INTRAC Conflict Management Workshop, November 1996).

In Liberia, a Children's Assistance Programme (CAP) for child combatants is supported by MSF-Belgium and the U N. The Children's Assistance Programme in Monrovia has re-integrated several hundred former adolescent warriors into Liberian society, focusing on ways of working with positive images of masculinity to assist boy ex-soldiers to find ways to be 'men' in a peaceful society.

It is important not to over-stress the role of development organisations in rehabilitation after armed conflict; communities themselves play the chief role in rehabilitation. Yet an interesting insight in Liberia is that some communities have their own way of reintegrating children back into society, through a ritual initiation or 'cleansing' process, not dissimilar to the initiation ceremonies for secret societies. This is one example of the way in which people are able to draw upon traditional institutions to deal with the consequences of war (Bradbury, 1995).

The pilot Stepping Stones programme in Buwenda, Uganda, is a training package designed to address 'HIV/AIDs awareness, gender issues, communications and relationship skills' among young men. The programme is a response to 'a need to address the vulnerability of women and young people in decision-making about sexual behaviour' (Welbourn 1995). Stepping Stones considers young men's self-image needs and identity, and questions of conflict and mediation. Issues considered include the pressures on men concerning money, tradition, alcohol abuse, peer pressure and social expectations. The programme recorded a decline in domestic violence and alcohol consumption after 16 months' community participation.

The UNHCR Women Victims of Violence Project in Kenya worked with police*men* to discover their views of women, of vulnerability, of violence and rape in order to develop co-operative strategies with refugee women for the reduction of rape and assault. (Gardiner, 1996).

Conclusion

This article has attempted to highlight the fact that, in situations of conflict, the failure to address men's gender interests and identities is potentially lethal. The socialisation of young men must be the next stage in gender analysis. Just as human needs theory contributed to development planning and practice, understanding gender-specific motivation, options, and choices may assist our strategies for breaking cycles of violence.

'Gender' as an area of research and action should be understood as belonging to men and studies of masculinity, as well as to women and feminist studies. The use of gender analysis for the formulation of development policy is at a critical stage. It is time to extend the simplistic analysis of gender in conflict explored at the start of this article to take on the complexities of the ways in which women and men, girls and boys, respond to situations of armed conflict.

The socialisation of boys and young men is of vital importance in understanding the causes of conflict, allied to a recognition of the structural factors which are creating conflict in resource-poor situations. Reclaiming positive cultural traditions of manhood alongside those of womanhood is an area of research in social theory that needs to receive more attention from development theorists and practitioners. In development and relief work, the entry point for these wide issues seems to be innovative work in counselling and rehabilitation which takes male gender interests and identities, and socialisation processes, into consideration. Support should be provided to communities in their efforts to re-integrate the survivors and perpetrators of armed conflict.

Judith Large is a Fellow of the Department of Politics and International Relations. She is an independent consultant focusing on conflict and grassroots peace-building.
Tel: (0044) 1453 757040
Fax: 751338 e-mail: jwl4@gn.afc.org

Notes

1 The terms 'masculinity' and 'femininity' refer to characteristics which shape, inform, or construct behaviour for reasons deemed by a given society; the 'values, behaviours and attributes which are culturally associated with the male and female biological sexes respectively' (Tunnicliffe, 1991).

2 Christopher McLean, author of *Men's Ways of Being*, suggests that these jostlings are visible in many societies quite early on:
In dominant masculine culture, the need to 'be somebody' is exaggerated and extreme. Competition and the struggle for power are central. One only has to observe young boys to see how central this is to their sense of self-worth. A simple walk turns into a constant competition — the first to the next corner, jumping the biggest puddle, throwing a stone further than anyone else, walking way out in front of everyone else. (McLean C (1995) 'Boys and education in Autralia' in *Dulwich Centre Newsletter* 213, London.)

3 *Andrew Metcalf's study of Hunter Valley miners has shown them claiming to be more masculine than owners and managers to compensate for their lack of power in the work place, while Paul Willis's conversations with the fathers of his 'lads' revealed that though society at large might see mental work as superior to manual and reward it accordingly, they boosted their self-esteem by equating mental with feminine.* (Jordan 1995)

Bibliography

Beijing 1995 Platform for Action Report.
Bennet, Bexley and Warnock (1995) *Arms to Fight: Arms to Protect*, Panos.
Bracewell, W (1995) 'Mothers of the Nation.' *War Report* 36, September.
Bradbury, M (1995) *Rebels Without a Cause*, Care Report on the Conflict in Sierra Leone.
Brett, R (1996) *Study on Child Soldiers.* Geneva: Quaker United Nations Office.
Byrne, B (1995) *Gender, Conflict and Development.' Vol. 1: Overview*, BRIDGE briefings on development and gender series. Brighton: IDS.

Chesoni, A (1995) 'Thoughts on sisterhood and solidarity.' *Wajibu*, 10: 4.

Duffield, M (1994) 'Complex emergencies and the crisis of developmentalism', *IDS Bulletin* 25: 4. Brighton: IDS.

Duffield M (1994) *Complex Political Emergencies with reference to Angola and Bosnia: an exploratory report for UNICEF*, School of Public Policy, University of Birmingham, UK.

El-Bushra, J and Piza-Lopez, E (1993) *Development in Conflict: the Gender Dimension*, Oxfam UK/Ireland-ACORD.

Enloe, C (1983) *Does Khaki become you? The Militarisation of Women's Lives*, Pluto.

Frankel, M (1995) 'Boy soldiers: turning killers into kids again' in *Newsweek*, 7 August 1995.

Gardiner, J (1996) Report on UNHCR's Women Victims of Violence Project, Kenya, for CODEP workshop, Oxford.

Gilmore, D (1990) *Manhood in the Making: Cultural Concepts of Masculinity*, Yale University Press.

Goodwin-Gill, G and Cohn I, (1994) *Child Soldiers: the role of children in armed conflicts*, Clarendon Press, Oxford.

ICRC Special Brochure (1995) *Women and War*, Geneva: ICRC Publications.

Jani, P (1995) 'The necessity of a reconciliation process in North Albania', *Anthropology of East Europe Review*, 13: 1.

Jordan, E (1995) 'Fighting boys and fantasy play: the construction of masculinity in the early years of school', *Gender and Education* 7: 1.

Large, J (1995) *The Work of Generations: Gender Analysis and Future Policy Directions*, CODEP.

Lockwood and Baden (1995) 'Beyond the feminization of poverty: gender-aware poverty reduction' *Bridge* in Brief September.

Moghadam, V M (ed) (1994) *Gender and National Identity*, Zed Books and Oxford University Press.

Mohamed, F (1996) speaking at the CODEP 'Beyond Working in Conflict' workshop at Oxford Brookes University, 4 — 6 November 1996.

Olonishakin, F (1995) 'Women and the Liberian Civil War' *African Woman* 10, September.

Purvis, A (1995) 'Beware the children' in *Time* 4 December

Richards, P (1995) 'Rebellion in Liberia and Sierra Leone: a crisis of youth?' in Furley (ed) *Conflict in Africa*, Tauris.

Satterwhite, J (1996) Unpublished report from fact-finding mission for Christian Peace-making Team of NGO's to Chechnya, April.

Thorne, B (1993) *Gender Play* New Brunswick, NJ: Rutgers UP.

Tunnicliffe, S (1991) 'War, Peace and Feminism: an Expansion of Galtung's Theory of Cultural Violence.' Presented at conference of British International Studies Association, University of Warwick, December.

UNICEF (1995) *State of the World's Children*.

Willis, P (1977) *Learning to Labour* Farnborough: Saxon House.

Wallace, W (1996) 'Sudan's rootless war children run wild', *The Observer*, 7 July.

White, S (1993) 'Making men an issue: gender planning for the "other half."' in Macdonald, M (ed) *Gender Planning in Development Agencies*, Oxfam.

See also:

Chevannes, B 'The Male Problem: An Afro-Caribbean Perspective', *Children in Focus*, 5: 2 (UNICEF).

The role of men in families:
achieving gender equity and supporting children

Patrice L Engle

Fathers and men in families represent one of the most important resources for children's well-being. Social services, including development interventions in the South, have hitherto failed to take into consideration the major role of men in families, and its effects on women, on children, and on the men themselves.

A recent UNICEF report concludes, 'If UNICEF is going to continue to contribute to development goals and gender equality...there will have to be greater efforts to involve men' (Richardson, 1995, p. 6). Similar concerns have been raised by the Ford Foundation, Save the Children, and many other NGOs. That men should be involved in reproductive health programmes was a major recommendation from the Cairo Conference on Population and Development. Despite this interest, social service and health programmes continue to target mothers and children, ignoring the role of men in the lives of children.

In recent years, most development interventions focusing on the well-being of the family have stressed the importance of the mother/child relationship, even in societies in which the father controls decisions about the household and family welfare. Economic instability, and the inability of institutions in both developed and developing countries to increase their contributions to families, have led to a search for additional sources of support for children (Bruce et al., 1995). The efforts on the part of the state, and many development organisations, to improve the welfare of children by increasing male income proved to be less effective than originally expected in terms of improving children's nutritional status and health (Marek, 1992).

Not only has the income of men not benefited children as much as expected; women are more likely to use their income for the well-being of children than are men (e.g., Jackson, 1996). Agencies have sponsored income-generating projects for women, and the provision of credit for poor women. However, while approaches which focus on women have had many benefits both for women and for children, there is considerable evidence that this focus may increase the workload of already overburdened women, reducing their personal well-being and their ability to care for their children (McGuire and Popkin, 1990).

This article surveys programme initiatives, conferences, research, and publications concerned with the role of men in the family, organised by agencies such as UNICEF, The Population Council, and the Consultative Group for Early Childhood Care and Development.

Social fatherhood

The concept of 'father' needs to be widened from a biological role to one which emphasises socialisation and support of many kinds during childhood. Although this nurturing aspect of 'fatherhood' is recognised across cultures, the person who plays the father role may or may not be the biological father. Responsibility for children may fall to the mother's brother; or older male kin such as the grandfather (Richardson, 1995). A 'social father' may take responsibility for all of the children a woman has, even though some were biologically fathered by another man. The narrow concept of 'father' could thus be appropriately replaced with 'men in families'.

Four of the major contributions men make to family life are: taking economic responsibility for children, building a caring relationship with children, reducing the chances of 'unpartnered fertility',[1] and ensuring gender equality in the family (Family Impact Seminar, 1995; Richardson, 1995). The absence of any of these will represent a problem for children's development; while taking such roles can enhance the lives of men. This new perspective has been seen as a threat by feminists and others who have struggled long and hard to bring women's issues to the forefront (Engle, 1995).

Fathers in families

The percentage of female-headed households in developing countries ranges from about 10 to 25 per cent, and has increased gradually over the last decade (Bruce et al, 1995). The highest rates of female head-

ship are reported in the African countries of Botswana (46 per cent), Swaziland (40 per cent), Zimbabwe (33 per cent), and the Caribbean countries such as Barbados (44 per cent) and Grenada (43 per cent). Some rates in the developed countries are equally high, ranging from 38 per cent in Norway, 30 per cent in Germany, and 32 per cent in the United States (United Nations, 1995).

Many of these statistics reflect patterns of family formation which differ from the Western model of a nuclear family. In Botswana, which has a high rate of female headship, mothers live with their natal families until their partners are well into their forties (many men are migrant workers in South African mines). Even though support is customarily provided by the mother's family, these families are still reported as female-headed.

However, residence of the father within the household does not always imply either an economic contribution to his family, or involvement with his children. In the Caribbean, for example, many men contribute to their children's upkeep, but have only a visiting relationship with their children's mother; whereas others may be co-resident in a household, but provide no economic support for the family due to poverty, lack of employment, or spending on alcohol or drugs (Brown et al, 1994). Research shows that if the presence of the father is to have a positive effect, this requires some involvement of the father with the child (e.g. Levine et al., 1993). Research and programme efforts need to look at the relationship between father and child, rather than just co-habitation.

Forces affecting the family

Two forces which may influence family formation and the role of men in families, are urbanisation, and changing patterns in women's employment, with underemployment of men. Urbanisation is characteristic of the industrialised regions of the world, which UN statistics cite as 77-78 per cent urban. South America is equally urban: rural, as is Northern Africa; and the rest of Africa and Asia are between 28 and 33 per cent urban (United Nations, 1995). Urban populations are growing in all areas, especially in sub-Saharan Africa and Asia.

The changing gender composition of the workforce in developing countries is likely to have significant effects for men's roles (Evans, 1995). In the past two decades, women's employment, as measured in national census surveys (primarily formal employment) has increased in all areas, except sub-Saharan Africa and Eastern Asia. In comparison, men's economic activity rates have declined significantly everywhere except central Asia (e.g., US 81 to 75 per cent, Latin America 85 to 82 per cent, Southern Asia 88 to 78 per cent) (United Nations, 1995).

Effects of fathers on children

Building a caring relationship and child-care
In the literature, 'father involvement' normally refers to the establishment of warm and close relationships between fathers and their children. This can be accomplished with relatively little time investment; the most important ingredient appears to be positive emotion and attention to children. Although infants initially show preference for mothers over fathers, infants become attached to their fathers by the end of the first year of life, even if the fathers spend relatively little time with them (Cox et al, 1992).

In the US and Europe, studies have reported that fathers who were involved with their children contribute greatly to their children's intellectual, social, and emotional development. Easterbrooks and Goldberg (1985) found that the quality of the interaction (the father's sensitivity to the toddler's needs) was a better predictor of the children's cognitive performance than the amount of time spent with the child.

For men in many parts of the world, to have a 'caring relationship' with an infant or young child is a novel expectation. For example, some participants at a seminar in Lesotho in 1991 felt that the interactions that African men have with very young children are rare, accidental, and of little importance. (Bernard van Leer Foundation, 1992).

For example, fathers in Zimbabwe, were surprised to learn that they 'should' play with their children from birth onward; they expected to wait until the children could talk. However, for older children, the pattern changes: in most African countries, fathers and grandfathers train older sons.

Fathers' time in infant and child care
Worldwide, fathers spend significantly less time in child care than mothers. Barry and Paxson (1971) summarised ethnographic reports from 186 cultures, and found that the percentage of cultures in which fathers had 'regular, close relationships' during infancy was 2 per cent, and 5 per cent in early childhood, although the percentage in which fathers were in frequent close proximity was much higher (32 per cent for infants, 52 per cent for young children).

However, some fathers do spend time performing child-care activities. Jahn and Aslam (1995) observed men living in squatter settlements in Karachi, Pakistan. In 75 per cent of observations of children being carried, the man was the carrier, even when the woman was present. How these patterns change with urbanisation and increased maternal employment (and decreased paternal employment) will be important to investigate; new expectations for father involvement may emerge if alternative providers of child-care are unavailable.

Effects on fathers themselves
One of the benefits of the changing roles for men in families is increased closeness to children. An extreme case is repres-

ented by men who take primary care for their children. This number is small, but is continually growing. These men often did not choose the role, but many express how much the experience has meant to them, and the importance of their attachment to their children (e.g., Davis and Chavez, 1995, for Hispanic men in the US).

Economic support for children

Female-headed households

A contribution to household income from fathers tends to be associated with improved child status; female-headed and maintained households with children are generally poorer than families with a male head, although there is considerable variation depending on the social and economic context of the female heads .

It is a truism in development circles that female-headed households are among 'the poorest of the poor'. This point has recently been questioned, in relation to the degree of economic poverty, but also in relation to the degree of access that such households have to decision-making within their communities and in wider society (Varley 1996). Certainly, children in female-headed households are not always worse nourished than those in male-headed households. Studies show that negative effects of female headship are seen in Latin America, but not sub-Saharan Africa (Desai, 1991).

Studies have shown that although the father's income may have a positive effect on food expenditures and child well-being, these effects may be smaller than if the income were under the mother's control (Hoddinott and Haddad, 1995; Buvinic et al, 1992). Women may be more likely to perceive children's needs, may develop stronger attachment to the child, and social roles may dictate that women are responsible for obtaining food for children (Engle, 1990).

In Kenya and Malawi, despite lower incomes, a smaller percentage of children in female-headed households were malnourished than in male-headed households (Kennedy and Peters, 1992). In Botswana, children in female-headed households received more education than children in male-headed households (Kossoudji and Mueller, 1983).

Costs of father's presence

The presence of the father is not always a positive force in either women's or children's lives. Women may improve their situation and that of their children by leaving an abusive partner. In a collection of studies of violence against women worldwide, rates ranged from 20 to 60 per cent (Heise, Pitanguy and Germain, 1994). It is possible that abuse of children is more common if a man is present in the family.

The cost to the family of the father's consumption of food and resources may be a drain on the family budget, particularly if he is not employed or is spending money on alcohol or cigarettes .

Avoidance of 'unpartnered fertility'

The third contribution that men can make to responsible fatherhood is to avoid sexual encounters which risk the birth of unplanned and unwanted children. Few cultures emphasise sexual restraint on the part of young males. Rather than encouraging the use of contraception and sex education to prevent the birth of unwanted children, traditional cultures attempt to protect young women through a combination of strict religious constraints on sexuality, or very early marriage (Richardson, 1995).

When pregnancies do occur, families may put great pressure on the couple to form a relationship. However, increased acculturation and urbanisation may undermine these supports. In a rural Guatemalan community, the rate of unpartnered fertility has doubled in the past decade, from 6 per cent to 12 per cent (Engle and Smidt, 1996). In the US, among teen mothers, 67 per cent of 'traditional' Hispanics were married, compared to only 44 per cent of 'non-traditional' Hispanics (Mirande, 1988).

Effects of gender inequality in the home

Gender inequality in the home, (i.e.men having a greater amount of authority in decision-making) has been associated with increased rates of domestic violence or restriction of life opportunities for women. Patriarchal control is often associated with low rates of schooling for girls, low status of women, early age of marriage, and high rates of malnutrition for children (Ramalingaswami et al, 1996).

Despite similar levels of income and health care services in sub-Saharan Africa and South Asia, rates of malnutrition in South Asia are almost twice as high. The authors explain this 'Asian enigma' as a consequence of the extreme subordination of women in South Asia: 'Judgment and self-expression and independence largely denied, millions of women in South Asia have neither the knowledge nor the means nor the freedom to act in their own and their children's best interests' (ibid., 15).

Ways forward: promoting committed fatherhood

International advocacy

International conferences — such as UNICEF's *Innocenti* Global Seminar (Richardson, 1995), and the Population Council's *Taller Para Padres Responsables* (Workshop on Responsible Fatherhood) (Engle and Alatorre Rico, 1994) — are opening the debate. The groundwork was laid for including men in reproductive health programmes at the Cairo International Conference on Population and Develop-ment (Richardson, 1995). Now many groups are including fathers in their plans. However, gender equity must be included in all these discussions.

Legal protection for children

Establishing protection for children of absent fathers may be quite difficult (Folbre, 1992). For example, in Mexico this lack of protection is due to the deficiency of Mexican law (Brachet-Marquez, 1992). Desertion is necessary in order to seek an award for child support, but is not recognised in law if the husband returns within six months. This means a man can come and go for years as long as he spends one night every six months at home.

If a husband chooses to stop paying to support his child, the burden of initiating legal procedures falls on the wife. Many husbands simply claim insolvency (ibid), and monitoring fathers' income is extremely difficult. The scarcity of employment in Mexico has resulted in more and more men earning untraceable non-wage money. Similar problems occur in other countries.

Promoting caring relationships

A community-based effort to build and support fathering skills has been remarkably successful in the Caribbean. The Caribbean Child Development Centre has established fathers' groups, which have formed an organisation called Fathers Inc. Fathers, who are often non-resident with their families, follow a curriculum to learn parenting skills (Brown et al, 1994). Reasons for the success of the groups are that they are men-only, and are initiated by men's interest in their children (Caribbean Child Development Center, 1994).

A second strategy is to bring fathers into schools and day-care centres, to help with child care. To be effective at building caring relationships, these programmes must increase fathers' interaction with their children, rather than simply allowing men to take part in the same activities as their children side-by-side.

Kavanaugh (1992) describes a project to create father and child nights at a day-care centre in New Mexico, USA. The success of the programme was attributed to balancing discussion with activities, promoting attendance by making contact with men face-to-face to invite them, having a male member of staff, and making a formal contract with the fathers to attend.

Levine et al (1993) created a manual promoting methods to encourage the involvement of biological fathers, or 'father substitutes', in pre-school programmes in the US for low-income children. Some of his suggestions include becoming aware of cultural limitation on the father role, providing men with a variety of ways of being involved, keeping open to various kinds of men in the child's life (e.g. grandfathers), and becoming aware of resistance both in the staff and among the mothers to men's involvement.

Experimental studies have shown that short-term programmes focusing on child development and fathering can have significant effects. Marked improvement was seen in the relationship of fathers to adolescents in Cameroon (Nsamenang, 1992), to newborns and young infants after prenatal education in the US (Parke et al 1979), and to pre-school-aged children after a ten-week father-only programme in the US (McBride,1991). These fathers reported feeling more responsible for daily decisions about their children, the kind of involvement which men are least likely to achieve. The most effective programmes were those which included mothers in separate training, since the changes involved both parents.

Combining fatherhood development and job-training skills
Because a primary cause of lack of support for children appears to be too many obligations for men, programmes in the US have attempted to increase low-income unwed fathers' payment of child support through combined job training, job placement, payment enforcement, and fatherhood education projects (e.g., the Public/Private Ventures Project, Achatz and MacAllum, 1994). Despite great difficulties in recruiting fathers into the programme, the results have been encouraging: child-support payments have increased, and men's feelings about themselves have improved (ibid). This programme included a component labelled the Fatherhood Development Curriculum. Once a week, the men in the project met to discuss issues of manhood and fatherhood, and consider the mother's perspective.

Educating children in broader gender roles
Education for children in responsible fatherhood is likely to have a lower (social and economic) cost than redressing current problems through direct re-education for fathers. Klinman (1986) developed a plan to give boys in junior high and high school (11-18) experience with young children through working in pre-school programmes. In many societies, young men are used as child-care providers as well as young women, and this helps their ability to nurture.

Establishing rights to paternity leave
Another strategy to increase father involvement is to promote child-care leave for fathers, either paid or unpaid, and flexible working hours. However, such opportunities are used by only about 10 per cent in the US and Sweden (Pleck, 1985). The low usage of paternal child-care leave may be due to prejudice by employers, the desire of the wife to stay at home, or possible loss of income for the father.

Father involvement at this stage also has the obvious benefit of alleviating the workload of mothers. An approach which had this aim was a Save the Children project in Vietnam (Richardson, 1995). Husbands were told that they could reduce the health-care costs for their children if their wives were to work less during pregnancy and immediately post-partum. In the communes which received the messages, women had significantly more rest days while pregnant, and higher birthweight babies, and men felt more empowered to help their wives.

Paternity as an issue for social services
As stated earlier, a bias noted frequently by researchers into fathering has been the exclusive attention to mothers and children within much of the health and social service literature. According to Bolton (1986), in the social service field in the US, men are either providers, the 'good guys', or they are not providers, in which case they are the 'bad guys'. There is little awareness that some men may choose to stay at home to take care of children, or may be unable to work due to unemploy-ment, lack of training, or disability. Social services need to recognise that many fathers are trying to meet their obligations; there are only a few 'bad' ones. They themselves may be in need of help; inability to meet the demands of being a provider often drives men away from paternal responsibilities. In health-care services, the role and signifi-cance of the father, which varies according to cultural context, needs to be understood if health-care provision is to be approp-riate and uptake maximised. The role of the father may be significant. For example, in the US the father's opinion was one of the most important indicators of whether a mother went for prenatal care (Sable et al , 1990) and breastfed. One recommendation from Pakistan is to develop a two-pronged approach, continuing outreach to women, but adding outreach to men (Jahn and Aslam, 1995).

In Vietnam, it was found that men had very little knowledge of UNICEF's 'Facts for Life'. UNICEF organised a contest for men, to survey knowledge of these issues, and write an essay. About 47,000 entries were received. In the months following the contest, oral rehydration therapy (ORT) use increased by 60 per cent, and child immunisation rose to 90 per cent. Grandfathers were particularly interested in increasing their involvement with children (reported in Richardson, 1995).

Encouraging paternal responsibility'

Following recommendations from Cairo, reproductive health programmes have begun to target sex education messages to men as well as to women. There is some concern that giving men the messages will simply disempower women again, after years of struggling to place reproductive control in the hands of women. Gender equity as well as increasing the role of men must be the focus.

There is also a growing attempt by governments to establish male paternity at the time of the child's birth. In one successful example in the US, almost two-thirds of unmarried parents voluntarily acknowledged paternity if they were provided the opportunity during the first few days postpartum (Family Impact Seminar, 1995).

Promoting gender equality

The strongest predictor of improved gender equity in the home is women's education (Richardson, 1995) and related income-earning. Thus, increasing access to education for girls has been a major focus of international pressure. In South Asia, women's combined disadvantages of lack of education, dowry, and young age at marriage (10-14) result in low status in the family. In Rajasthan, India, a UNICEF project promoted education for girls and delaying the age of marriage. As a result of two- or three-day visits and awareness-raising by a team of five women, who met with male village leaders and visited house-to-house, the number of adolescent girls in school increased, and the number of marriages decreased (Richardson, 1995).

UNIFEM and the Bahai church were able to change men and women's views about traditional male and female roles in Malaysia, Bolivia, and Cameroon through the use of drama and song, and consultation. Men were helped to understand the disproportionate workloads of women. As a result, spouse abuse and alcoholism have declined (Richardson, 1995).

Conclusions

At last, the critical role of men in families for the well-being of children, women, and of the men themselves is being recognised. Men's involvement in the 'private sphere' of the household and family is as crucial to economic and social development as the involvement of women in the 'public sphere' of income-generation and community decision-making. Furthermore, the two are interlinked: many successful development projects promoting women's participation outside the home have been aided by support from sympathetic men. In the absence of such support, the potential benefits for women, children and men themselves are jeopardised.

There are a number of techniques which can be used to support men in their parenting role while promoting gender equity in the home, but these issues must be linked. Perhaps the most effective will be those which are preventative, which work with the next generation of mothers and fathers to expand their roles and stress the importance of both parents' contributions. Following Barker et al's recommendation from Rio de Janeiro (1995), we need to support the non-traditional men who are striving to construct new role-models for themselves. The benefits to current fathers, to their partners, and to their children of their involvement with young children suggests that we must work in this direction.

Patrice Engle teaches at Cal Poly State University, San Luis Obispo, CA
e-mail: pengle@cymbal.aix.calpoly.edu

Notes

1 'Unpartnered fertility' is the procreation of children with a biological mate with whom the other parent does not have a social relationship.

References

Achatz, M and MacAllum, C A (1994) *Young Unwed Fathers: Report from the Field*, Phila, Pa: Public/Private Ventures.

Barker, G, Loewenstein, I, and Ribeiro, M (1995) 'Where the boys are: Attitudes related to masculinity, fatherhood, and violence toward women among low income adolescent males in Rio de Janeiro, Brazil', Mimeo.

Barry, H, and Paxson, L M (1971) 'Infancy and early childhood: Cross-cultural codes: 2', *Ethnology* 10, 466-508.

Bernard van Leer Foundation, (1992) 'Where have all the fathers gone?' *Newsletter 65*.

Bolton, F G (1986) 'Today's father and social services delivery system: A false promise', in M E Lamb (ed) *The Father's Role: Applied Perspectives*. New York: John Wiley.

Brachet-Marquez, V (1992) *Absentee Fathers: A Case-based Study of Family Law and Child Welfare in Mexico* PC/ICRW working paper series. *Family Structure, Female Headed and Maintained Families and Poverty*.

Brown, J, Bloomfield, R, and Ellis, O (1994) *Men and Their Families: Contributions of Caribbean Men to Family Life*, West Indies: Sprectrum Graphics.

Bruce, J, Lloyd, C B, and Leonard, A, with Engle, P L, and Duffy, N (1995) *Families in Focus: New Perspectives on Mothers, Fathers and Children*, New York: Population Council.

Buvinic, M, Valenzuela, J P, Molina, T, and Gonzales, E (1992) 'The fortunes of adolescent mothers and their children: The transmission of poverty in Santiago, Chile' *Population and Development Review* 18, 269-297.

Caribbean Child Development Centre, School of Continuing Studies (1994) *Men and Their Families: Discussion Guide for Use by Groups in Church, School, Community and Other Settings*, Kingston, Jamaica: University of the West Indies.

Cox, M J, Owen, M T, and Henderson, V K (1992) 'Prediction of infant-father and infant-mother attachment' *Developmental Psychology* 28, 474.

Davis, S K, and Chavez, V (1995) 'Hispanic househusbands', in A M Padilla (ed) *Hispanic Psychology: Critical Issues in Theory and Research*, Thousand Oaks: Sage (pp. 257-287).

Desai, S (1991) *Children at Risk: The Role of Family Structure in Latin America and West Africa*, New York: Population Council Working Papers No. 28.

Easterbrooks, M A, and Goldberg, W A (1985) 'Effects of early maternal employment on toddlers, mothers, and fathers' *Developmental Psychology* 21, 774-783.

Engle, P L (1995) 'Mother's money, fathers' money, and parental commitment: Guatemala and Nicaragua', in R Blumberg, C A Rakowski, I Tinker, and M Monteon (eds) *Engendering Wealth and Well-being*, Boulder, Colo:Westview (pp. 155-180).

Engle, P L (1995) *Men in Families: Report of a Consultation on the Role of Males and Fathers in Achieving Gender Equality*, New York: UNICEF.

Engle, P L, Hurtado, E, and Ruel, M (1995) 'Smoke exposure of women and children in highland Guatemala: Measurement Issues'. Submitted for publication.

Engle, P L (1993) 'Influences of mothers' and fathers' income on child nutritional status in Guatemala', *Social Science and Medicine* 37: 11, pp.1303-1312.

Engle, P L and Alatorre Rico, J (1994) *Taller Sobre Paternidad Responsable (workshop on responsible fatherhood)*. The Population Council/International Center for Research on Women Technical Paper Series, May.

Engle, P L, and Breaux, C (1994) *Is There a Father Instinct? Fathers' Responsibility for Children*, New York: Population Council Series.

Engle, P L (1990) 'Intra-household allocation of resources: Perspectives from psychology' in B L Rogers and N P Schlossman (eds) *Intra-Household Resource Allocation* (pp. 63-79). Tokyo: United Nations University Press.

Engle, P L and Smidt, R (1996) *Consequences of Women's Family Status for Mothers and Daughters in Guatemala*, Technical Report, The Population Council, New York/International Center for Research on Women Series (also to be translated into Spanish and published).

Evans, J (1995) 'Men in the lives of children', *Coordinators' Notebook* 16, 1-20.

Family Impact Seminar (1995) *Disconnected Dads: Strategies for Promoting Responsible Fatherhood*, Washington, DC: Family Impact Seminar Background Briefing Report.

Folbre, N (1992) 'Rotten kids, bad daddies, and public policy'. (Paper for the International Food Policy Research Institute-World Bank Conference on Intrahousehold Resource Allocation, Washington, DC)

Heise, L, Pitanguy, J, and Germain, A (1994) *Violence Against Women: The Hidden Health Burden*, World Bank Discussion Paper 255. Washington DC: World Bank.

Hoddinott, J and Haddad, L (1995) 'Does female income share influence household expenditures? Evidence from Cote d'Ivoire', *Oxford Bulletin of Economics and Statistics* 57: 1, 77-96.

Jackson, C (1996) 'Rescuing gender from the poverty trap', *World Development* 24: 3.

Jahn, A and Aslam, A (1995) 'Fathers' perception of child health: A case study in a squatter settlement of Karachi, Pakistan', *Health Transition Review* 5: 2, 191-206.

Kavanaugh, J (1992) 'Getting daddy involved', *Bernard van Leer Newsletter* 65, 10-11.

Kennedy, E and Peters, P (1992) 'Influence of gender of head of household on food security, health, and nutrition', *World Development* 20: 8, 1077-1085.

Klinman, D G (1986) 'Fathers and the educational system', in M E Lamb (ed) *The father's Role: Applied Perspectives* (pp. 413-428), New York: John Wiley .

Kossoudji, S and Mueller, E (1983) 'The Economic and demographic status of female-headed households in rural Botswana', *Economic Development and Cultural Change* 31, 831-859.

Levine, J A, Murphy, D T, and Wilson, S (1993) *Getting Men Involved*, New York: Scholastic.

Marek, T (1992) *Ending Malnutrition: Why Increasing Income is not Enough*, World Bank Africa Technical Department, Population, Health and Nutrition Division, Technical Working Paper No. 5, October.

McBride, B A (1990) 'The effects of a parent education/play group program on father involvement in childrearing', *Family Relations* 39, 250-256.

McGuire, J S and Popkin, B M (1990) *Helping Women Improve Nutrition in the Developing World: Beating the Zero Sum Game*, World Bank Technical Paper number 114.

Miller, B C and Bowan S L (1982) 'Father to newborn attachment behavior in relation to prenatal classes and presence at delivery', *Family Relations* 31, 71-78.

Mirande, A (1988) 'Chicano fathers: Traditional perceptions and current realities', in P Bronstein and C P Cowan (eds) *Fatherhood Today: Men's Changing Role in the Family* (pp. 93-106) NY: John Wiley.

Nsamemang, B A (1992) *Human Development in a Third World Context*, Newbury Park: Sage.

Parke, R D, and Neville, B (1987) 'Teenage fatherhood', in S L Hofferth and C D Hayes (eds) *Risking the Future: Adolescent Sexuality, Pregnancy, and Childbearing* (pp. 145-173).

Pleck, J (1985) *Working Wives/Working Husbands*, Beverly Hills, CA: Sage.

Ramalingaswami, V, Jonsson, U and Rodhe, J (1996) *The Asian Enigma: The Progress of Nations*, 10-17. (NY: UNICEF).

Richardson, J (1995) *Achieving Gender Equality in Families: The Role of Males. Innocenti Global Seminar, Summary Report*, Florence, Italy: UNICEF International Child Development Centre, Spedale degli Innocenti.

Sable, M F, Stockbauer, J W, Schramm, W F and Land, G H (1990) 'Differentiating the barriers to adequate prenatal care in Missouri, 1987-1988', *Public Health Reports* 105: 6, 549-555.

Thomas, D (1990) 'Intra-household resource allocation: An inferential approach', *The Journal of Human Resources* 25, 637-664.

Todd, H (1996) *Women at the Center: Grameen Bank Borrowers after one Decade* Boulder, Colo: Westview.

United Nations (1995) *The World's Women 1995: Trends and Statstics* New York: United Nations.

Varley (1996) 'Women heading households: some more equal than others?' *World Development* 24:3.

Violence, rape, and sexual coercion:

everyday love in a South African township

Katharine Wood and Rachel Jewkes

A research project with pregnant teenagers in an African township revealed widespread male coercion and violence within sexual relationships. If reproductive health interventions are to be effective, practitioners need to be aware of the level of gender inequity and powerlessness women experience in particular social contexts and design interventions which challenge male violence.

In the past decade, sexuality has become an important area of research and development intervention, in response to concerns about reproductive health, notably the spread of HIV/AIDS, and concerns about fertility control and global population growth (Ulin 1992). The predominant focus has been on educating women, through sexual health programmes, to use contraception, and particularly condoms, as ways of controlling their fertility and protecting reproductive health (Dixon-Mueller 1993). However, health promoters frequently discover that although they can generate high levels of awareness and concern among women about contraception and sexually-transmitted diseases, including HIV/AIDS, they are much less successful in getting women to change their sexual practices.

In this paper we present findings of anthropological research in an African township in Cape Town among pregnant teenagers. Although the original scope of inquiry of the study concentrated on contraceptive use, bodily reproductive knowledge, and pregnancy, the emergence of violence as a central issue in informants' narratives led us to focus more on sexual dynamics within adolescent relationships.[1]

All but one of the informants interviewed described assault as a regular feature of their sexual relationships. We discuss the implications of these findings for promoting healthy sexuality. All too frequently, health promotion interventions fail to acknowledge sexual encounters as sites in which unequal power relations between women and men are expressed. It is these power relations which determine women's ability — or inability — to protect themselves against sexually transmitted disease, pregnancy and unwelcome sexual acts. In the context of unequal power, it is invariably men who determine the timing of sexual intercourse and its nature, including whether a woman should try to conceive, and whether or not condoms will be used.

Power relations between men and women take multiple forms, but in South Africa they are commonly manifested as and imposed through sexual violence and assault. An estimated 1.3 million rapes take place each year (*The Times*, 1997). This background of violence as a part of everyday life worsens the problems faced by women in negotiating about sexual activities, as possibilities of resistance are more limited, and the consequences of trying to resist are potentially very serious.

Male control over sexuality

Among the informants interviewed, it was usual for male partners to define the conditions and timing of sex. At the outset of the relationship, the men encouraged their partners to understand teenage love affairs as necessarily involving penetrative intercourse: as one adolescent woman explained, 'he told me that if I accept him as a lover we have to engage in sexual intercourse, and do the things adults do.' If girls accepted male requests to establish a liaison, the agreement 'to love' here, as in other parts of South Africa where we have undertaken research, was equated specifically with having penetrative intercourse and being available sexually. This equation appeared to derive from the men, who were reported to have explained that sex was the 'purpose' of love and that people 'in love' must have sex 'as often as possible'. Relationships were often contractual in nature, with the girl being expected to have penetrative sex when the man wanted it in exchange for presents of money, clothes, school fees, and food.

In most cases, the young women reported that men used violent strategies from the start of the relationship, forcefully initiating partners who often had no awareness about what the sex act involved: 'he forced me to sleep with him in his home, he beat me, made me take off my clothes, then made me lie on the bed and forced himself on top of me. It was very painful.' Many girls reported that they attempted resistance, but had felt forced to submit to the demands when assault was threatened or carried out: 'he told me that if I didn't want to do it, he would force me to. He beat me up and forced my underwear down.' These findings are in line with other recent research in South Africa, which asked girls about the circumstances of first intercourse. This found that 30 per cent reported that they were 'forced' to have sex the first time (Richter 1996, Buga 1996, Jewkes 1997).

Repeatedly, the language of the girls' narratives was of compulsion: 'he made me', 'he just pushed me and overcame me', 'he forced himself onto me', 'he did as he wanted with me', 'what could I do?' Our informants stated that in the absence of sexual knowledge on their part (which could potentially have been provided by female peers but was not), their ignorance was reinforced by the male partners who reportedly refused to explain what was about to occur. For example, one girl had asked her partner what he would do, and had received no answer except 'you'll see'. One teenager who was 11 years old when she first had sex described how, after the event, 'I met a friend of mine who told me to stop crying, and promise not to tell my mother or anyone else, she told me that all the girls my age to do it, that I should go home, clean myself up and keep quiet about what happened.'

Men continued using physical assault to enforce the contract, beating their partners if they refused to have sex, with belts, sticks, and shoes, often until visibly injured: as one teenager said, 'they don't care, they'll hit you anywhere, face and all. You'd think they would at least avoid that, because your parents will see the bruises and the injuries, but they don't care.' Physical assault was so commonplace that women stated that many of their female peers saw it as an expression of love: some of the informants used phrases such as 'he forced me to love him', and 'I fell in love with him because he beat me up', which expressed this contradiction. In some cases, violence was said to be the main reason why the girl continued to have sex; in the words of one informant, 'I continue because he beats me up so badly that I regret I said no in the first place.'

The extent of assault in adolescent relationships has been demonstrated in other research; in a study of 600 pregnant and non-pregnant teenage women in Cape Town, 60 per cent said that they had been beaten by the male partner (Jewkes 1997). The pregnant group, on average, reported having been beaten more that ten times during their average of two years of sexual activity (Jewkes 1997).

Men also controlled the relationships in other ways. Several girls described how their partners had torn up their clinic contraceptive cards in anger that they were using contraceptives; thus for some, even protection against pregnancy in the form of 'invisible' hormonal methods appeared to be non-negotiable.

Informants reported being beaten not only when they tried to refuse to have sex, but also when they were seen talking to another man on the street, when they informed the men that they wished to terminate the relationship, and when they were suspected of sexual infidelity. On this last point, it was normal for men to sustain double standards, taking multiple sex partners for themselves, while disallowing their regular girlfriend from even speaking to other men. Female refusal to submit to sexual demands was interpreted by men as a sign that girls had other sexual partners and were 'worn out'. Some informants reported control over them being enacted and reinforced by brutal means; gang-rape of adolescent girls by the man's friends was reported to happen 'often' in the community, as a way of 'punishing' them for actual or suspected

infidelity (a practice which has been widely reported anecdotally elsewhere in South Africa).

Awareness of unequal power

Since violence was perceived to be very common among married and unmarried people alike (and is very likely to have been witnessed in the home context), it was accepted as an inevitable part of relationships. The South African teenagers interviewed were generally aware of the power inequalities and double standards operating within constructions of love and sex, but resistance was complex in the extreme because of male violence, and peer pressure. As one girl explained, 'as a woman you have no rights, you must keep quiet and do as the man wants'.

In Jewkes' study, of the 60 per cent of teenagers who had been beaten, only 22 per cent of pregnant teenagers and 28 per cent of the non-pregnant control group said that they had in the past left a boyfriend because of assault (Jewkes 1997).

Interactive models of sexuality

The degree to which women are able to control various aspects of their sexual lives is clearly a critical question for health promotion. Our research was a fairly small and exploratory study, yet it underlines the need for issues of gender power to be considered in the design and impact assessment of HIV/AIDS and reproductive health interventions.

To date, many of these programmes have promoted the use of the male condom, based on a 'knowledge leads to action' model. The condom is seen as a simple protective device to be introduced into the sexual act at the 'right' moment. This implies that the individual is an independent person who can make decisions regardless of the opinions and behaviour of others, and of the wider social context (Campbell 1995). This ignores the realities of power dynamics, not least of which are the gender inequities which structure heterosexual relations. The fact that the degree of empowerment for women in their sexual lives varies widely according to context points to the need for specific, detailed, situational analysis as part of the development of locally useful interventions. It is strikingly evident from our research, and confirmed by other South African research, that women commonly find themselves wholly unable to negotiate the timing of sex, and the conditions under which it occurs. Many of them feel powerless even to protect themselves against pregnancy. Condom use is far from being a possibility in their sexual lives.

The implications for health promotion are clear: an understanding of difference derived from local analysis, and reinforced by a comparative perspective, is essential for interventions to be useful. As researchers from the AIDS and Reproductive Health Network in Brazil have observed: 'strategies of health promotion for women in especially acute situations of sexual oppression or violence cannot be the same as for women whose cultural or social setting offers them more effective means for the negotiation of sexual and reproductive practices' (1995, 7).

The questions which need to be considered in designing appropriate interventions include:

- How, why and when are decisions made by individuals to have sex, and to engage in specific sexual practices?
- How are gender inequities played out and resisted in the community? For example, how far are practices such as condom use and female sexual refusal negotiable and negotiated between individuals in different settings?
- How is individual control asserted when there is conflict?

Violence: an issue for men

Although gender violence is recognised internationally to be a common feature of women's daily experiences (Beijing Platform of Action 1995), most of the literature discussing health and sexuality completely fails to recognise the implications of violent domestic contexts.

In this South African setting, in which extreme disempowerment of women is portrayed, it is apparent that for development interventions promoting healthy sexuality to focus only on women would be wholly inadequate. The focus should be widened to consider the issue of gender violence, and male behaviour. Male violence against women is a major problem across the world, while South Africa is considered to have one of the highest rates of a country not at war. Although the definition of abuse varies across societies, cross-cultural research does indicate that 'virtually wherever the issues have been researched, a massive, under-recognised burden has been unveiled' (Heise 1994: 1176). Four recent survey-based studies in sub-Saharan Africa, for example, demonstrate that 46 per cent of Ugandan women and 60 per cent of Tanzanian women reported being regularly physically abused; in Kenya and Zambia the figures were 42 per cent and 40 per cent (Heise 1994).

There is a danger of non-governmental organisations (NGOs) neglecting work with men. In fairness, in view of the mismatch between the scale of the problem of domestic violence and the scant resources available for work to promote its eradication, it is not entirely surprising that NGOs working in the field in South Africa have predominantly concentrated on providing crisis support for female victims though counselling, refuges, or help with court interdicts. Many organisations do not work with men either as perpetrators or as victims of rape, because they prefer to allocate their scarce resources to women. However, there is a risk that in so doing, they may be unwittingly promoting the idea that violence is a 'women's issue', and suggesting, even though most NGO workers recognise this to be false, that if a woman can be removed from one violent context, with the necessary empowerment, she will be able to prevent abuse of her body in future.

Our research suggests that there is a need for NGOs to move beyond crisis management to reducing the prevalence of violence by engaging with men as perpetrators or potential perpetrators and recognising the contexts of abuse within sexual partnerships. Not only should gender violence be made a focus of sexuality intervention programmes, but attention should be shifted towards changing the attitudes and practices of men.

Incorporating men into gender programmes

Work on gender issues, both research-and intervention-oriented, has long been equated with work with women, without adequate recognition of the relational and contextual aspects of their lives. Men have been largely ignored. The main consequence of this omission in the work of NGOs and the health services has been a set of assumptions about women's ability to control their bodies and thereby achieve and sustain sexual health: assumptions which have significantly limited the impact of interventions.

Within the South African context we can more confidently identify the (currently neglected) potential of sexuality interventions which could be aimed at men, rather than give examples of current good practice, partly due to our own limited experience in the NGO arena. Our research has provided pointers which we hope will be further developed by both the education sector, and NGOs working with young people. There is clearly a need to work

with pre-adolescent children; in terms of developing alternative patterns of interpersonal interaction and reducing levels of violence in the country as a whole, this age group is crucial.

Basic needs for information must be met, including in the areas of reproductive biology, contraception, sexually transmitted diseases including HIV/AIDS, and condom use. Our research has found that adolescents of both sexes lack this information, or alternatively have information which is inaccurate or imbalanced.

Adolescents also need education on the many meanings of love and sexual relationships. Our research has shown that adolescent girls want to be able to have relationships which do not involve sexual intercourse, but are unable to do so because this is the dominant model of male-female interaction. One of the factors associated with violence in adolescent relationships, which affects both sexes, is poor communication skills and a lack of specific vocabulary with which to discuss sexual experience and desires. These skills also need to be developed at an early age, and are vital if verbal communication is to replace physical violence in relationships.

Interventions based on participatory techniques such as workshops, theatre, and games, can enable communities to develop awareness and skills in this area. One example of a training manual for community workshops on HIV/AIDS and communication and relationship skills which uses participatory methods is Alice Welbourne's programme Stepping Stones (1995) which has been used successfully in sub-Saharan Africa in particular.

Another example of a participatory intervention used by community workers is developed countries is Man's World, a small-group game for young men, which focuses on issues of masculinity and sexism and was developed by the B-Team (Resources for Boyswork) in Britain (1993). Development interventions like this which focus on building self-esteem among children of both sexes are valuable, since research repeatedly reveals an association between low self-esteem among men, and physical abuse of women. Similarly, developing attitudes of respect for personal autonomy, particularly of women, is essential.

The challenge is to put these ideas into practice. There is no doubt that if sexual health programmes are to become more effective in bringing about real change, there is an urgent need for them to take the lead from recent research on sexuality and domestic violence, and incorporate men fully into their focus. Unless the spotlight shifts towards men, health promotion initiatives in the field of sexual health will continue to be inadequate.

Katharine Wood and Rachel Jewkes are based at the Women's Health research focus of the Medical Research Council, Private Bag X385, Pretoria, South Africa.
E-mail <rjewkes@hoopoo.mrc.ac.za>

Notes

1 In-depth semi-structured interviews were conducted in Xhosa with 24 pregnant adolescent women, recruited and interviewed in the township Midwife Obstetric Unit to which they had come for antenatal care. The age range was 14 to 18, with an average age of 16.4 years, and most had male partners about five years older.

References

AIDS and Reproductive Health Network (Brazil) (1995) 'Gender, sexuality and health: building a new agenda for sexuality research in response to AIDS and reproductive health' (Unpublished).

B-team (Resources for Boyswork) (1993) *Man's World*, London: Resources for Boyswork.

Buga G, Amoko D, Ncayiyana D (1996) 'Sexual behaviour, contraceptive practice and reproductive health among schooled adolescents in rural Transkei', *South African Medical Journal* 86 (5): 523-527.

Campbell C (1995) 'Male gender roles and sexuality; implications for women's AIDS risk and prevention', *Social Science and Medicine* 41 (2): 197-210.

Dixon-Mueller (1993) 'The sexuality connection in reproductive health', *Studies in Family Planning* 24(5).

Heise L, Raikes A, Watts C, Zwi A (1994) 'Violence against women a neglected public health issue in less developed countries', *Social Science and Medicine* 39 (9): 1165-1179.

Jewkes R, Maforah F, Vundule C (1997) 'A case-control study of factors associated with teenage pregnancy in peri-urban Cape Town' (Data being analysed).

Richter L (1996) 'A survey of reproductive health issues among urban Black youth in South Africa'. Final grant report for Society for Family Health.

The Times, 5 April 1997, London:UK.

Ulin P (1992) 'African women and AIDS: negotiating behavioural change', *Social Science and Medicine* 34 (1).

Welbourne A (1995) *Stepping Stones: a training package on HIV/AIDS, communication and relationship skills*, London: Actionaid.

Wood K, Jewkes, Maforah F (1995) *Sex, violence and constructions of love: adolescent relationships in a Cape Town township*. Medical Research Council technical report.

'Crabs in a bucket':

reforming male identities in Trinidad

Niels Sampath

This article describes some of the ways in which 'masculinity' is understood. Looking at the example of a community in the Caribbean, it suggests that social changes can offer opportunities to deflect men's identities away from damaging patriarchal stereotypes.

The Concise Oxford Dictionary defines 'masculine' as 'characteristic of men,...manly, vigorous,...having qualities considered appropriate to a man'. This definition does not allow for conceptions of masculinity differing according to context. Instead, through suggesting that there is a single, logical, and unquestionable idea of what is 'masculine', the definition reflects the dominance of the Western concept of masculinity.

The publication of this edition of *Gender and Development* is just one example of how the notion of 'masculinity' is currently asserting a presence in the analysis of societies and their progression in the world. When dealing with both gender and development issues, one cannot, as has often been done, simply take masculinity and its apparently problematical patriarchal values for granted (Gilmore 1990). As one investigates different cultures and communities, each of which is continually changing over time, one begins to realise that men's voices, often reflecting different identities, are far from homogeneous. While some men may claim to be superior to women, they may also provide evidence

of a real fear of, or actual experience of, domination by women (Spiro 1993).

Both masculinity and femininity are cultural constructs and not universal human 'essentials'. Both are formed from 'bits and pieces of biological, psychological, and social experiences' (Levant and Pollack 1995, following Pleck 1981). This fact is accepted for femininity. Few, if any, books or journals are titled *'Femininity and [insert topic of choice]'*. Even as a plural, 'femininities' seems unpopular. Instead, women's changing or changeable *identities* are stressed, usually in a positive sense. By contrast, the stereotypes associated with the Western idea of 'masculinity' seem to have marked it down as the underlying reason for much that is wrong with the world.

Attempts at promoting 'new' male identities (for example, the Western 'New Man' in all his permutations) are often ridiculed or derided. While some women may say 'I am not a feminist, but...', some men will utter a similar phrase: 'I am not a male chauvinist, but...' (Morgan 1992:11). And for every committed feminist, there are many women who, implicitly or explicitly and in both major and minor ways, support the general male domination ideology, or *masculinism* as Brittan (1989) has termed it, and will reject men and women who do not ascribe to it.

The conclusion to be drawn is that many men, as well as women, feel a sense of entrapment within perceived stereotypes, whether the stereotype's alleged agenda is 'good' or 'bad'. In reality, people tend to 'mix and match' and, to use a Caribbean term, 'creolise' definitions and concepts to suit their own personal circumstances even if they are unable to articulate or effectively react against any social discomfort they feel.[1]

Although gender analysis is almost unavoidably set within a framework of largely Western-developed sociological gender theory, there is every reason to suppose that the same discomfort with, and occasional resistance to, stereotypes also occurs across semi-industrialised societies and those undergoing Westernisation or modernisation (Berreman 1973:23).

Masculinity with or without patriarchy?

What is meant by 'masculinity'? Gender issues are primarily issues of personal identity, set within the contexts of cultural and social definitions of sexual role. Whenever the term 'gender' is used, it is important to remember that one is not dealing with just a bi-polar concept of male *or* female identities. Within a culture or society, an individual can be faced with different desired, expected or fulfilled roles within a life-time. The level of pressure to conform to these gender roles is not entirely uniform over a life-time for anyone. Gender identities held by women and men can be submissive, complementary, or dominant to each other, depending on factors such as age and status. In this sense, gender identity can often seem, to the individual and community concerned, almost independent of the other sex.

Until recently, masculine identity has tended to be subsumed into studies of 'patriarchy' and its effect on society and women in particular, rather than studied for its own sake. This model is often quite far removed from non-Western or non-academic thinking about gender and sex which people in most developing communities assume and value. It also ignores the social importance of critical but subtle variations within 'masculinity', many of which work against men. I would argue that this makes it less likely that constructive patterns of change will occur through development interventions.

Caribbean men's 'reputation' and 'respectability'

Trinidad is an island in the Caribbean that, although best-known for African-Caribbean culture, is in fact quite multi-ethnic. South Asians, or East Indians as they are known, form the largest ethnic group. In addition, the economy is based on oil, and this industry has undergone dramatic boom/bust cycles in the last quarter-century since independence. As one can imagine, these conditions have produced a high degree of social and economic change. In particular, race and gender relations have been challenged by changes in the labour market and increased opportunities for women. With these changes have come strains on what had been considered to be 'traditional' gender relations and masculine identities. (In the following description I have italicized local expressions and they should be read as such.)

Women-centred studies and development programmes have paid attention to the common double-standards facing the emancipation of women (sexual and otherwise). African-Caribbean masculine identity, although often reinforcing that double-standard, faces a duality of its own in terms of man-to-man interaction. Wilson (1969; 1973) originally outlined West

Indian *reputation* and *respectability* characteristics that are key aspects of male identity.

Respectability involves those moral decisions and actions that are seen as positively influenced by European colonialism and the local pyramidal social structure based on class and colour. *Respectability* is a concept reflected by the norms of local genteel femininity: church-going and being 'well-behaved'.

Reputation is a working-class, live-for-today enjoyment of the kind of hedonism that is deemed as *worthless* by the respectable sections of local society. It is a male reaction to *respectability* (Littlewood 1993), and also acts as a control upon men and women who aspire to be respectable when they are locally deemed to be nothing of the kind (Wilson 1969). Honour is given. Honour is taken away.

The local analogy is made to crabs in a bucket: before any one individual can escape and because of the posturing going on within the bucket, that individual is dragged down by the others. Individuals in the 'bucket' of poverty and subservience in colonial or post-colonial society struggle to achieve the *respectability* that is assumed to exist outside their strata of society. As suggested above, going to church on Sunday is one way of beginning this process. However, in the meantime they have to survive within the crowded and extroverted community.

Members of each gender nominally involve *reputation* as their stratagem. For men, this usually takes the form of overt sexual banter and bravado. Women delve deeply into the nuances of party-going and local concepts of fashion. The tactics of both sexes stress individual consumerism and extroverted display.

In line with this, both men and women, but especially men, superficially tout the idea that it is a free society: free for the individual to do as he or she pleases. A strong *reputation* which emphasizes personal 'freedom' is deemed important in the post-slavery, post-plantation, post-colonial environment. Having been the perceived perks of the colonial elite, heightened consumerism and fashion are recognised

Creating contrast and enhancing masculine reputation by dancing *outside* a respectable wedding ceremony

Niels Sampath

as socially-constructed patterns of attainment of freedom. And freedom is seen to be necessary to ensure success on a day-to-day basis, since it allows one to *move well,* as is said locally. One is unshackled from perceived social constraints and one can conduct social business on a wider scale, not subservient to any other individual. However, even with the possible exception of some sports heroes and heroines, it is rare for men, as well as women, ever to reach a serene level of *respectability* by simply enhancing their *reputation* in this way.

Behaviour that enhances *reputation* is the anti-thesis of *respectability.* If people are seen to aspire to leave the 'bucket' they are branded as *too bright,* or *too high.* For example, in an urban Trinidad factory setting described by Yelvington (1995), the two characteristics define 'idioms of masculine control over women'. Men do not pass up an opportunity to test and verbally probe women's attempts at virtuous *respectability.* For in doing so, and almost no matter what the outcome, men enhance their own *reputation* among other men. According to Yelvington (op.cit.) *reputation* has a 'symbolic violence' which follows a continuum from gentle flirting called *sweet talk* through to less acceptable but more aggressive methods of power enforcement such as spreading malicious rumours or *mauvais langue.*

In such a traditional urban work situation women are left in a no-win situation balanced between either submitting at some point to male advances or engaging in deflective banter, usually in the form of returning the teases and taunts. In the first instance, they have plainly submitted, and in the second instance, they deny themselves *respectability* by reinforcing *worthless* male *reputation.* While some women may succeed for a while in taking a third course of action, i.e. ignoring male advances, the reality is that many women choose not to put themselves in the situation at all by avoiding the workplace altogether. In this way, the 'symbolic violence' of men trying to achieve a *reputation* effectively keeps women in the 'bucket' of social subservience. Again, it should be noted that the values encompassed by *reputation* and *respectability* can be endorsed, explicitly and implicitly, by both men and women, to themselves, as well as to each other. The 'crabs in the bucket' analogy appears to apply to both genders at all levels.

Yet, at this point it must be stated that the above qualities have supporters, detractors, and 'conscientious objectors' amongst local people of both sexes (as do femininity, feminism, male chauvinism, and the New Man syndrome elsewhere). It is among this plurality of experience and opinion that opportunities for reform and development may be found. A more rural and youthful example further illustrates the point.

In my own fieldwork study in a rural Hindu East Indian village in Trinidad, for every professional flirt such as could be found in the urban factory, there was a hopeless romantic who was socially paralysed by a self-imposed boycott to avoid 'trying to *sweet-talk* women into this and that'.

Tabanka pertains especially to young village men: the word describes social belittlement, and sexual and moral shame. It is usually applied to male African-Trinidadians when a woman's affections are lost to another man (Littlewood 1985). Indian adolescents (and here one must include all unmarried men as well as teenagers) have few opportunities to engage in active heterosexual relationships. So the term *tabanka* has been extended by them to include the common state of unrequited love. Here a *macho reputation* has, for one reason or another, been prevented, rather than lost. In this respect, the effect of the mocking which customarily accompanies their predicament is different.

A 24-year-old individual known as Pastor, who was once an enthusiastic Christian convert who had mocked Hindu idolatry, found himself longing for, though not speaking to, a young woman hairdresser in the village who was rumoured to have broken off with a boy from elsewhere. Pastor gave up *liming* (hanging out) with his *pardners* so that he could walk back and forth in front of her house, hoping for something spontaneous to occur. His *pardners* in turn intensified his *tabanka*: by belittling his situation (and the woman) and telling him to 'make a move on the chick man, she's an old cat'.

Instead, Pastor sought solace in watching Indian films on videos where, for example, after years of separation, the hero and heroine might actually speak to each other before a painful death. He began re-attending Hindu prayer meetings. If he went shopping for his family, people would ask him if he was going to buy *gramazone*, a defoliant commonly used as a suicide potion.

While Pastor's ex-*pardners* made light of his situation, Pastor attempted to console himself with the relative security of more traditional 'Indian culture'. Lack of 'modern' masculine success and not *moving well* can be indicated by a reversion to fatalism and a relative over-concentration on traditional sources (the domestic sphere, dominated by women, is seen as the haven of traditional culture). To quote one of Pastor's *pardners*:

Poor Pastor. He does want to make a move on the girl but he ain't gettin nowhere. He used to mock them star-boys in Indian films and now he suffering just like they. Well, that is what does happen. Once you does lose courage to take action, bang, tabanka does take hold and you back sitting and scratching, doing nothing.

Pastor, it seems, could not be blamed for being attracted to the girl, but he could not successfully broker the dominating cultural values involved. According to his *pardners*, had he not mocked traditional Indian values in the first place and partly retained their security he might have had the courage he sought to establish a successful 'masculine identity'.

Based on the Trinidadian urban and rural examples, the problem it seems, is that 'masculinity' is based on local perceptions of 'success'. Just as women are socially valued as 'sex objects', so men are valued as 'success objects' in a context of *reputation*. The two values appear to complement each other within a patriarchal paradigm. The question then becomes, how does one begin to escape that paradigm?

Re-forming male identities

While it may appear as if gender relations are trapped in a static web, there are possible ways forward. Because the local criteria of value as sex or success objects for both sexes are quite narrow, they tend to produce many variations of excluded or compromised values and individuals, which then quietly incorporate themselves within the creolised environment of, for example, multi-ethnic Trinidad. The unfortunate key word there is 'quietly'. As in our own society, 'alternative' culture is often used as a defining contrast for that which is largely hidden from the mainstream. By and large, there is still a paucity of acceptable varieties of expression of masculinity in day-to-day activity within most national cultures. But often the potential for change is already well in place.

In Trinidad and the Caribbean, one has the process of *creolisation*: a mixing within the accepted values of the dominant constituents. This takes place not just between attributes of race, religion, or ethnicity, but between any opposing or corresponding social characteristics on all levels, gender included.

Miller (1994) points to a more positive analytical future partly because he effectively discusses Trinidadian gender issues without making them his absolute focus. He refers to a less gender-laden duo of social characteristics he calls the 'transient' and 'transcendent'. In some ways these still reflect *reputation* and

Posing for passers-by

respectability. But Miller's analytical terms apparently sort through the rest of society and return to the gender puzzle without being trapped within masculinism's terms of reference. He makes a useful contrast between carnival and Christmas.

Trinidad carnival is a hedonistic free-for-all that tests the boundaries and allows for creative expression that is both male and female. The action is on the street and non-domestic. The past has passed and the future is tomorrow, and for a few days neither matters. In that sense, the carnival is an event which emphasises transience.

By contrast, Trinidad Christmas is, quite apart from Christian religious aspects, a national cultural marker where various influences are appropriated for future recall through family and long-term relationships. In its *respectability* and location in the domestic female domain, Christmas transcends day-to-day life. Yet, neither

Christmas nor carnival would be quite the same without the other; and each ensures the other's survival.

What is interesting is that there has been a perception in Trinidad that 'women are [gradually] taking over carnival'. The first indication of this was noted in the 1950s by Powrie (1988[1956]), but since then it has accelerated. Some carnival bands have a ratio of ten women for every man. There are several reasons for this.

To begin with, women in Trinidad, while hardly emancipated to their own satisfaction, have nevertheless made some strides in that direction. But their near predominance in Trinidad carnival is due to more than a simple trend. Carnival acts as an escape valve, a time when notions of traditional *respectability* do not apply. The difference between everyday life and carnival is greater for women than for men.

Indeed, some women say: 'men in Trinidad, they think every day is carnival. But women must think of work.' And so, women are more enthusiastic about carnival. Ironically, many women can maintain 'traditional' concerns about clothes and make-up, and domestic gossip through carnival, but now it can be done extra-domestically and with a greater cultural purpose that they feel legitimises these activities to the masculinist, paternalistic society in general.

There are also economic reasons for women 'taking over' carnival. Men have traditionally been employed in plantation and heavy and manufacturing industry. These activities are in decline. The service sector, including those economic activities maintaining carnival itself, is the growth area, and here women predominate, and are making significant progress into middle-management. Thus, women are increasingly likely to be the steady income earners and are invariably in charge of domestic finances. As a result, women can set money aside specifically for carnival bands and fêting, whereas many men, who feel obliged to try to 'party' (or *lime* as their get-togethers are known) on a constant basis, are invariably short of the required cash.[2] As women have involved themselves with carnival, they have injected it with a transcendent quality to the point where it is now a year-round preparatory industry.

In the rural East Indian village where I did my fieldwork, a similar shift has occurred whereby what was once some-what *transient* — the existence of increasingly independent women — has become more *transcendent*. Within the space of a few years, families were no longer looking for semi-arranged marriages for their young men to girls who could simply be mothers and 'didn't want to work'.[3] Instead, a good education and a steady job have become something that young girls actively seek out. While young men drop out of school and complain that there are no jobs to study for, young women seem to be less pessimistic (or perhaps less socially able to do anything outside the home other than study or 'take courses').

The economic circumstances affecting urban life have also affected the life of the village. Traditional sugar plantation work has declined dramatically as has higher-paid work in the oil industry. At the same time local (non-plantation) agriculture and related sales and distribution, in which women have always had significant involvement, are part of the new growth in the service industries. While 'service' has connotations of subservience, unlike traditional industry where physical labour was important, a *reputation* as sought by men, is of little value any more.

In both urban carnival and rural community life, it could be said that women have had less motivational investment in the 'crab in the bucket' analogy. That has always been a primarily male concern. Indeed, academic criticism of Wilson's theories stresses that the notion of the relegation of women from the public sphere, so that they can uphold a 'colonial respectability', is itself both Eurocentric in its framework and ignorant of several areas of women's public interaction (Besson 1993; Douglass 1992).

Women have, perhaps, found other means of escaping from the 'bucket' than dragging others down. They have utilised the transient (carnival) and immediate economic necessity (things that men might use for themselves to enhance their *reputation*) to develop more permanent ways of escape from subservience.

Men have had to adjust their identities accordingly and at least try to delete that component of male success which insists that women cannot also enjoy 'success' in relation to their own. This may not always go smoothly and might initially seem impossible. But in every sphere of life in the Caribbean, the diaspora population, both African and Indian, male and female, has *always* had to make changes to 'tradition'. Changes to male identity would not be a new experience.

Development and male identity

Research into the effects of patriarchy on women has been relatively thorough, but this may have deflected attention away from the fact that men are dominated by other men, and are denied alternative expressions that could be more benign to women. It is only with a recognition of the potential for a range of identities that *the effect by men on men as well as women* can be appreciated. Recruitment to progressive changes should then be easier. It is less socially divisive if men and women are dedicated to the same project.

As I have illustrated using the example of Trinidad, different feminine and masculine identities can exist despite an apparently monolithic stereotype. Unlike the exclusivity of power and status which is suggested by the traditional notion of patriarchy, an inclusive tendency can be fostered given certain conditions. Inclusivity, or 'non-crab-in-a-bucket' behaviour, appears to be intrinsic in those areas where women have contributed to development.

However, with regards to men, constructive and inclusive conditions may be missed or not considered if the initial focus is purely on interactions between women and men, rather than on intrinsic masculine/feminine identities. By examining men's identities more closely, development decisions could promote the positive aspects of masculine identities, assisting *both* women and supportive men in the creation of less patriarchal societies. The 'problem' with masculinity is not masculinity itself, but how it is focused.

Niels Sampath is a research student at Oxford University.
address: 20 Russell Court, Woodstock Road, Oxford OX2 6JH, UK.
e-mail: niels@lofgren.demon.co.uk

Notes

1 The *Concise Oxford Dictionary* defines 'creolise' as 'make [the] (language of [the] dominant group, in [a] modified form) into [the] sole language of the dominated group.'
2 See also Rodman (1971:172—173).
3 In Trinidad, the dowry system did not survive the migration from India.

References

Berreman, G D (1973) 'Self, situation, and escape from stigmatized ethnic identity', in Brogger, J (ed).

Besson, J (1993) 'Reputation and respectability reconsidered: a new perspective on Afro-Caribbean peasant women', in Momsen (ed). Brittan, A (1989) *Masculinity and Power*, Oxford: Basil Blackwell

Brogger, J (ed) (1973) *Management of Minority Status*, Oslo: Universitetsforlaget.

Douglass, L (1992) *The Power of Sentiment: Love, Hierarchy, and the Jamaican Family Elite*, Oxford: Westview Press

Gilmore, D D (1990) *Manhood in the Making: Cultural Concepts of Masculinity*, London: Yale University Press.

Hearn, J and D Morgan (eds) (1990) *Men, Masculinity, and Social Theory*, London: Routledge.

Levant, R F and W S Pollack (eds) (1995) *A New Psychology of Men*, New York NY: Basic Books.

Levant, R F and W S Pollack (1995) 'Introduction', in Levant and Pollack (eds) op. cit.

Littlewood, R (1985) 'An indigenous conceptualization of reactive depression in Trinidad', *Psychological Medicine* **15**, 278—281.

Littlewood, R (1993) *Pathology and Identity: the work of Mother Earth in Trinidad*, Cambridge: Cambridge University Press

Miller, D (1994) *Modernity: An Ethnographic Approach: Dualism and Mass Consumption in Trinidad* London: Berg.

Momsen, J H (ed) (1993) *Women and Change in the Caribbean: A Pan-Caribbean Perspective* London: James Currey.

Morgan, D H J (1992) *Discovering Men* London: Routledge.

Pleck, J R (1981) *The Myth of Masculinity* Cambridge, MA: MIT Press.

Powrie, B E (1988) [1956] 'The changing attitude of the coloured middle class towards carnival', in K Johnson (ed) (1988).

Spiro, M (1993) 'Gender hierarchy in Burma' in Miller (ed) 1993

Wilson, P J (1969) 'Reputation and respectability: a suggestion for Caribbean ethnography', *Man* (NS) **4**, 70-84.

Wilson, P J (1973) *Crab Antics* New Haven: Yale Univ Press.

Yelvington, K A (1995) *Producing Power: Ethnicity, Gender, and Class in a Caribbean Workplace* Philadelphia PA: Temple University Press.

Gender workshops with men:

experiences and reflections

Kamla Bhasin

During the last few years I and my colleagues have conducted workshops with men — mostly senior men, in decision-making positions in NGOs. This article focuses on my experience of the first six of these: two were in India, two in Bangladesh and two in Nepal. My colleagues and I felt confident, both as facilitators/trainers, and as feminists, to handle this task.[1] As development activists we now had enough experience of work at different levels, as trainers we were well equipped and confident, and as feminists we were less angry, less emotionally charged and less confrontational; we felt we could manage a useful and sustained dialogue with men on sensitive issues.

It was around 1990 that I first heard demands for workshops on women's issues for men. These came from different quarters, for different reasons. Rural women said they were now quite aware of women's issues, and it was time that their men were given a proper 'brain-wash' (*dimaag dhulai*). In contrast, women activists and development workers wanted workshops with men because they saw increasing tensions between men and women workers within NGOs. They were dissatisfied with, and more articulate about, subtle and open discrimination against women within NGOs, and felt 'charity must begin at home'.

As a response to the increasing awareness of women's issues, several donors started suggesting 'gender sensitisation workshops for men' for NGOs supported by them.

Some of us women who were involved with training and keen to challenge patriarchy within development organisations also recognised the urgent need to have a dialogue with senior male workers and decision-makers from voluntary organisations.

Although these days everyone can make some 'correct' statements on women, most NGO leaders have not yet critically examined their own behaviour and attitudes towards, and assumptions about, women.

My willingness to have a dialogue with men on women's issues is based on my belief that men can and must change their thinking, attitudes, and behaviour *vis-à-vis* women, specially if they want a more just and equitable society. I believe that it is necessary for women to challenge or persuade those men who are our partners in different struggles and movements, to reflect on women's issues; without a common understanding and shared commitment to change gender relations, it is difficult to work with men (or with women) at home, in organisations, and in movements. I also start with the assumption that if, I as a middle-class person, can work with and in the interest of the working classes, men can work with and in the interest of women for a society without gender hierarchy.

The purpose of gender workshops for men

Our approach to gender workshops with men is broad-based; we have tried to make the workshops integrative and holistic. The objectives of the workshops are:

- to develop an understanding of gender and gender relations in the contexts of other divisions such as class, caste, and North-South divide;
- to create an atmosphere which encourages the participants to reflect critically on their own understanding of gender relations and gender issues and on their attitudes and behaviour;
- to help participants to analyse the nature of development policies and programmes in general and those of their own organisation in particular, in terms of their impact on women, ecological sustainability, and equity;
- to collectively evolve a vision of an equitable and gender-just family, community, and society and to develop a strategy for its realisation;
- to create a network of like-minded people and organisations.

As in all training sessions, I begin by affirming the participants, trusting them and believing in their capacity to change, however painful the process of change may be. In every workshop we try to make men talk about their personal lives and experiences, their personal relationships with women at home, in the work-place, and in society at large, to make them realise that, unlike other issues, gender can not be dealt with merely as an intellectual discourse. Changing gender relations challenges each one of us to reflect critically on ourselves and to change, if necessary.

Workshops in Bangladesh, India, and Nepal

All six workshops had 15 to 20 (men) participants, they lasted four to five days, they were all residential, and all were held in quiet and very simple places away from the distractions of city life.

In three out of six workshops we found that several senior men who had agreed to participate did not attend, and did not give any reason for their absence. Some of us wondered if this might be because our focus was on women's issues. Serious classes and study groups are seen to be necessary for understanding issues like class, caste, community organisations, environment, even account keeping, and office management; yet they are not considered necessary for women's issues. 'What is there to learn on women's issues?' seems to be the attitude.

It is this attitude which is the major hindrance in the way of serious reflection on the issues.

Reassuring the participants

Our first task in these workshops was to dispel some of the anxieties, insecurities, and hostility that [male] participants bring with them. Since almost all of them were attending a workshop on gender for the first time, some were quite anxious, and a little insecure; they were not sure how to respond or behave. Their insecurities and anxieties perhaps also stemmed from the fact that for the first time both the facilitators and trainers were women — and women who were well-known as feminists, development workers, and trainers, and as strong and confident people. During the first few hours of our interaction we hear remarks like:

> 'So, now we are in your hands...'
> 'We are ready to be butchered!'
> 'We have come to be brain-washed!'
> 'So, are you going to convert us?'
> 'You should really not bother to train men, because it is you women who are your own enemies!'

These statements came in spite of our best efforts not to be provocative. But the very fact of inviting men to a gender workshop is provocative, especially for those men who know that a discussion on women's issues will raise uncomfortable questions about matters which are normally not addressed! We found that participants who came from large and hierarchical organisations, and who were in senior decision-making positions, were the most insecure, and, therefore, most hostile.

Starting with the personal

We begin every workshop with personal introductions where everyone is asked to speak about his family background, present family status, his organisation, and his own work. We also ask them to tell us about their expectations of the workshop, and the issues they would like to discuss.

After this, we briefly discuss the importance of personal introductions. Getting to know each other well, we explain, is the basis for developing a common understanding and creating solidarity; and in order to know each other well, we have to see each other as a 'whole'; we have to break down the usual compartments between the 'personal' and the 'official', between the private and the public.

Starting with the personal also gives everyone a chance to speak, and to build a confidence that everyone has something to share and to give. It helps to create an atmosphere of warmth, closeness and equality. At the same time, it gives an idea of where each one of us is starting from, and what areas we would like to discuss and explore. This makes it easier to plan the workshop, and the level of discussion.

Clearing the ground

In order to avoid misunderstandings, we begin by saying that we do not look at gender issues in isolation; we see them in the context of larger, economic, political, social, and cultural systems and we believe that changes in gender relations would require changes in other social systems, and vice-versa. In this context, we inform them that our own past and present involvement and experiences have been not only with women's issues, but also with issues related to poverty and development, caste, class, environment, human rights, and so on. We also clarify that we look at women's subordination as a system, and therefore for us it is not a question of men versus women.

We also make it clear that we neither have ready-made answers for everything nor do we believe in dishing out the 'correct line' or solutions. We ourselves are searching for answers and this search, will and should be an on-going, dynamic search.

The issues

Although the final list of issues discussed at these workshops is prepared in consultation with the participants, the issues tend to be similar in every workshop and they are the following:

- The situation and position of women and men in our society.
- The concept of gender.
- Patriarchy as a system and an ideology and the origin of patriarchy.
- Analysis of development policies and programmes in terms of their impact on ecology, on the poor, [especially on women] and on the Third World.
- Analysis of NGO structures, policies and programmes from the perspective of women.
- Feminism and the women's movement.
- Vision of a society without gender and other hierarchies.
- Strategy for sustainable and gender-just development.

On every issue, our attempt is to move from social realities to generalisations and concepts.

In order to get everyone to speak, we encourage small-group discussions of the issues listed above. As resource persons, our task is to fill in the gaps in the discussions, add our views as and when necessary, and provide conceptual and theoretical outputs. On issues with which the participants may not be familiar, or on which they may have the wrong notions (according to us!) we do not hesitate to give lectures. Such issues are likely to be patriarchy, feminism, gender, the women's movement, and feminist analysis of development.

In all the six workshops, we found that the participants were well aware of, and quite articulate on:

- women's double burden of work ;
- the active participation of working-class women in production, and their contribution to household incomes;
- the lack of participation by men in child-rearing and household activities;
- the widespread discrimination against girls and women in matters of food intake, health care, and education;
- the lack of participation of women in major decisions within the family and in all decisions in the community.

The participants generate empirical data in group discussions on the subordination of women within and outside the household. It is also easy for them to see how official development programmes — and also most NGO programmes — have been male-planned, male-executed, and male-oriented.

Some difficult issues

The problems arise when we try to draw conclusions based on the information they provide. This is when we sense a certain uneasiness, resistance and hostility.

To give an example: to explain the position of men and women in the family — the most intimate and crucial social unit of all — we ask the participants to put on the blackboard all the oppression women and men may suffer within the family. The women's column gets quickly filled. Each participant can suggest something — female foeticide, female infanticide, sexual assault, psychological harassment, control over women's work and income, discrimination in providing health care, education, and so on.

The participants have to think hard to point out the oppression men face within the family. They can only come up with things like 'they are not allowed to cry', 'they also have to submit to stereotypes', 'they have to look after the women', and so on. However, many participants get extremely upset when we conclude that the family can be the location of injustice and discrimination against women. We have been accused of 'wanting to break up peaceful families', and 'attacking local culture'. During these discussions, we often find men becoming very insecure, and as a result extremely defensive about the family. They express fears about the disintegration of the family (which would of course mean loss of authority, comfort, and power for them).

We encourage the participants to reflect on their own reactions. We argue that removing the prevalent inequalities and injustice within the family, can actually strengthen rather than weaken it. We also encourage them to look at the family from the point of view of women. We provide a historical view to show how in every society the institution of the family has been changing in response to changes in the mode and relations of production.

Men questioning patriarchy

Some men find it difficult to cope with the concept of patriarchy. They are ready to describe atrocities against women, but they resist looking at them as a system. Some of them say: 'you can describe women's oppression, but you don't have to see it as a well-thought-out and planned system. We men are not *that* vicious'.

One standard response to looking at women's subordination as a system is that it came to India because of and in response to foreign invaders. 'We Indians had to subjugate our women when the Muslim invaders came'. (As if women in India were free as birds before that!)

Another very common response is — if there is a problem, it is created by other women. The 'woman is woman's worst enemy' theory is supported with real-life examples of mothers and daughters in-laws. Men who readily analyse caste and class as systems seem to be too afraid (or too intellectually dishonest?) to consider patriarchy as a system.

A third response is often in the form of a question: 'If you are against patriarchy, are you for matriarchy? Is that the solution?'. To help the participants to see beyond hierarchies, we invite them to consider the possibility of equality between the sexes (equality, not sameness, because another accusation made in these workshops is 'you feminists want to be like men').

Some participants feel relieved by being able to put the blame for everything on an abstract system. But to avoid complacency and stress personal responsibility, we emphasise that all systems are maintained by individual actions.

Feminism: much misunderstood

In most workshops, the largest number of questions are about feminism and the women's movement:

- Isn't feminism or the women's movement imported from the West, and isn't it alien to our culture and religion?
- Isn't feminism confined to 'five-star elite' women who have no idea of the lives and issues of poor, rural women?
- Why is feminism confrontational?

Won't it destroy the most important unit in society, i.e. the family?

Although we face such questions all the time, we must confess to surprise and disappointment when NGO leaders, who have been working for women's development for years, share all the usual misconceptions about feminism and the women's movement. We had hoped that at least the senior staff would be better-informed, and would have thought seriously about these issues.

We normally ignore such allegations on the first three days, and take up these loaded issues only after establishing a degree of rapport and some understanding of women's oppression, women's development, and so on. We realise that it would be futile to reply to such questions with ready-made answers. Instead, we ask participants to list the issues which have been raised by South Asian feminists, and examine them one by one to see which of them are Western, and so irrelevant to India; which are urban and not relevant to rural women; which are elite women's issues and therefore irrelevant to poor women.

The board gets filled quite fast with a list of issues — dowry, rape, sex-determination tests, female foeticide, equal wages for equal work, property rights, land rights, alcoholism, ecology, unionisation of self-employed women, job reservations, child-care, sexism in media, pornography — the list is unending! Even a cursory look at these issues shows that none of them is Western and most of them are related to working-class women. Issues like dowry, sex determination tests, or pornography, which might have been confined to the middle class earlier are no longer so today.

After dealing with misconceptions about feminism and the women's movement, we discuss why such misunderstandings exist, even among sympathetic men.

In four workshops, we asked the participants who had said things like 'all feminists are urban, middle-class women, with no understanding of the local culture', to substantiate their statements by giving examples. In each case, we found that the statements had little factual basis, but were based on general discomfort with feminism, or on some anti-feminist propaganda in the media. In two cases the anti-feminist sentiments were based on a single encounter with 'an aggressive woman' or 'a woman who believed in smoking'.

The only plea we make when we face such generalisations is that judging a large movement by the behaviour of one or two women is obviously neither accurate nor fair. We also explain that, for many of us, becoming a feminist is a long, arduous journey; none of us are perfect, nor do we have well-thought-out positions on everything. Few of us practise all we preach. In this, we are no different from socialists, Gandhians or environmentalists.

Workshops and masculinity

How are these workshops different from those with women? There are obvious differences: the level of personal sharing is much greater in an all-women workshop. Women are more prone to talk about their personal experiences while men are much more guarded.

We find that men are quite happy to deal with abstract and impersonal theory, but they have little experience of talking about themselves and their emotions. They seem to suffer from the 'brave boy', 'strong man' syndrome. Men can quite easily talk about the subordination of poor women, but are often unwilling to look at their own families. They seem trapped in a terrible insecurity, anguish, and fear of the family structure collapsing, their position disappearing from under their feet.

We realised that for women, talking about themselves is easy and also a release, because they feel oppressed and seldom find a supportive atmosphere to talk about their experience. It is much

more difficult for men to look at themselves as some one who is privileged, who might be oppressing his wife or sister consciously or unconsciously or who enjoys the advantages of being a man. We encouraged men to talk about their experiences as a son, husband, father; whether they thought they enjoyed privileges which women did not have, what they felt about that. Did they ever reflect on the gender differences within the family? Discussions were never really focused or intense. We are not sure if this was due to lack of time, poor planning, our inability or resistance from the participants.

In contrast, women's workshops are very intense and emotional. In almost every workshop some women break down while talking about the discrimination they have faced, the oppression or neglect they have suffered. Men resist making a shift from the mind to the emotions, from the public to the personal. The rare male participant who is keen to explore his personal relationships does not find many male partners, and ends up discussing these issues only with us women.

Another difference is the subtle resistance by men to looking at women's subordination as a system. Women, on the other hand find it liberating to look at their subordination in this way. Naming the system, and assessing it dispassionately, is the first step towards dismantling it. It is in the interest of women to name and change the patriarchal system, but it is not so for men and hence there is resistance and defensiveness among men regarding patriarchy, especially to discussing it in their own personal context.

Women training men

In spite of over 20 years experience and our abundant grey hair, it is difficult for some men to accept us as resource persons or to accept our authority; to admit that we could teach them something. Men who consider themselves leaders are very hesitant to admit that they have not studied or thought seriously about the issue. Some of them constantly intervene, try to divert the issue, bring in irrelevant matters, in an attempt to disrupt, making it difficult for us to remain calm.

The women resource persons are perhaps also considered to be 'interested parties'. The fact that it is easier for men to accept male authority became quite obvious in one of the workshops when on the fourth day a male observer came and spoke eloquently about religion and culture being most oppressive for women. Everyone listened to him in great silence, while we had been heckled for saying things half as strongly. This and other similar experiences have made us realise that as women trainers we have to learn to use power and authority judiciously.

We feel it might be good to have a sensitive male as a co-trainer, someone who can speak as a man, have a 'man-to-man talk' if necessary, and who will not be seen as an interested party. A man in the trainers' team may also blur the divide which exists between women trainers and men participants.

We need to tread gently

We need a far more sensitive approach to the way men are oppressed by gender. We have to realise that men who try to break certain gender roles also pay a price; and one must try to feel the same sympathy for their oppression, and not constantly trivialise it by comparing it to women's. It is difficult to look at men's oppression under patriarchy seriously and sincerely, without depoliticising or diffusing the issue of women's subordination. We have no easy answers.

As trainers, we have to be much more patient, detached and non-committal in a workshop with men. We should also not be too confrontational. Much against our nature, we think we perhaps have to learn to be circuitous, to take one step forward and another sideways. After all, the purpose of these workshops is to make allies, and not more enemies.

Improved understanding, and a desire to move towards better gender relations, is evident when, towards the end of the workshop, the participants discuss their future strategy for women's development. What they come up with is clear, comprehensive, and concrete. The written evaluations done at the end of every workshop are overwhelmingly positive. Most participants state that they learnt a lot, they were forced to think things through, they were challenged to reflect on their beliefs and behaviour. At every workshop they recommend that such workshops should be mandatory for all men working in development organisations.

We do not succeed in winning over all the men. With one or two, the tensions never subside. These men are unable to accept women as trainers, and are not open to admitting that they may need to revise their attitudes. If developing a feminist understanding and consciousness is a long, painful process for women, it will be much longer and more painful for men. These workshops can only be the first step of a long journey.

(A version of this paper was published by the International Council of Adult Education in *Convergence* XXIX;1, 1996)

Kamla Bhasin is Co-ordinator of the FAO – NGO South Asia Programme and is based in Dehli. E-mail: FAO-IND@field.fao.org

Notes

1 By 'we', I mean myself and women like Vasantha Kannabiran (India), Khushi Kabir (Bangladesh), and Meena Acharya (Nepal) who have been my partners in workshops with men.

New masculinity:

a different route

Gonzalo Falabella G

This article formed part of a presentation made by the Chilean sociologist Gonzalo Falabella at the First Citizens' Forum for Tolerance and Non-discrimination, which took place in Santiago de Chile in March 1995. The subject arose out of the experiences and conversations of a group of professional men, who were searching for a new identity.

These ideas come from a group of Chilean and foreign men who have been meeting for two years, monthly. They came out of our attempt to take a new approach to life. The initiative arose out of a weariness with some aspects of our lives, such as the excessive hours we work; our sense that we seek power because it is intrinsically interesting to possess it; the lack of real intimacy between male friends, and our habit of reducing our conversation to politics; the tricks that life holds in store for you; and work. 'What do you do?' is interpreted by men as a question which purely focuses on work. We are dissatisfied with the lack of attention that we give to our personal lives, our marriages and our families, no matter what stage of life we are at.

Competition, unpleasant 'machismo', the power vice, and a lack of personal sensitivity are all the norm for men, and all are both influenced by, and in their turn influence, the fate of this country. As men, we would like to live in a less isolated way. However, our environment makes this increasingly difficult.

The writings of Robert Bly — in particular his book *Iron John* (Bly 1991) — had a great influence on the group, especially initially. His statement that women are marked out for pain, whereas men are distinguished by not showing their sorrow, not weeping for their problems (because, in fact, 'men don't cry'), struck home with us. We saw the need to create our own forum, in which men who had a common desire to share their feelings could find mutual support. Throughout our journeying, our female companions have helped us, often without realising it, by just allowing us to watch them get on so well with their own struggles, supporting and loving each other to the extent of inciting our envy!

In time, we were creating our own masculine identity, a 'new man' in the Chilean style. We agreed at the first meeting that we were not just a group of friends, nor a support group, nor a therapy group, nor one which only wanted to respond better to our feminist comrades and their challenges. When we met a week ago — two years after the group was first formed — we defined the group simply as 'a forum where we can comfortably share our experiences'. We are professional men who wish to know ourselves, and our women, better. This wish extends beyond our sense of status which is based on our parentage, identity, and political opinions. We aim to lead more fulfilling lives and become more complete, less isolated men.

The sources of the search

There are several sources for our search. First, the women's movement has helped to raise the consciousness of men, in Chile and elsewhere. More recently the 'men's movement' (especially in the USA) has begun to search for an alternative to traditional masculinity.

Many different philosophical influences — including Jungian and Eastern thought, Mediterranean mythology, and myths of the Chilean native people — recognise a more integrated vision of men and women, and of 'male' and 'female' aspects of human personality. These ideas of human nature allow both sexes to gain self-respect, and allow a more diverse and integrated development process for men and women.

Likewise, research on the matriarchal stage through which our societies passed (for example, Arroba 1996) has shown how positive this period was for humanity. Studying this period opens the way for us to design a future society where the inclusion of women in power is seen as beneficial to society.

We are also influenced by Marxism. In its original concept of social democracy, Marxism sees society governing itself as a political objective. Social democracy overcomes the limits of representation by others, to allow everyone to deal with the direct government of his or her own society. This means different social classes and strata must be enabled to participate, regardless of the area in which they live, ethnic origin, class, sex, educational status, or age. Understanding how all these aspects of social identity affect people's ability to participate allows men to recognise, and work to change, gender relations, in solidarity with women.

The basis of inequality

As men we would like to say that the way we are is not due to mere ill-will, or a masculine conspiracy to overshadow women in society. There are social structures and institutions which reproduce unequal, hierarchical, authoritarian relationships between the sexes. It is a culture based on intolerance. However, in these same relationships, it is also possible to find new 'signs of the times' which show ways of overcoming the negative aspects of these relationships. In our view, inequality between women and men in our society is based on the following:

First, the traditional family is an institution where male violence and authoritarianism is reproduced. It also establishes extreme differences in the roles of women and men, and emotionally castrates the male child. We feel that the Catholic church, and its fundamentalist vision of spirituality perpetuates many of the oppressive relationships and values of the family.

In Chile, the system of the 'hacienda' (estate or ranch) is a vertical and authoritarian structure of total domination by the landowner over his representative, by the representative over the superintendent, by the superintendent over the foreman, by the foreman over the tenant farmer, and his oppression of his wife, her of the children, and they of the dog! Today, after almost 20 years of dictatorship and an entrenched 'hacienda' culture, which is even present in the basics of trade union legislation, many of these relationships, with a modern veneer, can still be found in companies that may possess modern machinery, but retain archaic working practices, recently denounced by the Minister of Employment himself. Much is spoken about 'total quality' today in Chile, but it is never more than talk, which few put into practice.

The military is another powerful forum for promoting male authoritarianism, and an anti-democratic national security. The armed forces uphold the rigid control and social relations of an earlier time.

Traditional schooling (though teachers are now less respected by society), with its lack of respect for the student's dignity, reduced freedom, artificial differentiation between the sexes and maintenance of sexual segregation, is another source of conservatism in our society. This kind of education does not produce young men or women with progressive values, or stimulate creativity and innovation.

The state also contributes to the creation of gender inequality. In Chile, women only got the vote in 1949. The state is prejudiced against people who are differentiated from the norm; for example, in every corner of the country, the state is disdainful of the ability of people in the regions: '... we need to develop their skills to reproduce central commands', says one official statement. This is an affirmation of the different situations of subordination to which we have referred, of which the subordination of women is a key example.

However, in each of the institutions mentioned above, there have recently been signs of a breakthrough, however small, against authoritarianism, rationalisation and 'machismo' (male chauvinism).

Some paths to follow

How do we respond as individuals to the above issues? We would like our personal development as men to go beyond mere rivalry. What we are hoping to be able to do is to find a substitute for competition as a way of relating to each other. We believe that our search is part of a movement to create a country that is more just, more tolerant, and where people work in solidarity. Our own struggle as men is part of a wider battle to create 'a better country', in the last words of Allende.

We would like to take pleasure in the positive aspects of our male identity. We are convinced that sexual equality in all fields and the development of our own sensitivity will create more fulfilling lives and better relations within and between the sexes, both in work, politics and society. We would like to achieve gender relationships which do not disintegrate into inequality in the home, work, society and politics.

There appear to us to be three ways to achieve our development as more integrated men. Firstly, we have to learn to be intimate with each other as men, within our group. Secondly, we need to increase our level of intimacy with our partners. To begin with, we can do this by radically redefining our roles, emphasising our role in the care of our children and, through that, enabling us to have a closer relationship with them. Thirdly, we need to relate these issues to wider social struggles outside ourselves and our families. The object is to untie the hard knots in society's fabric which have been tied by authoritarian institutions. The new masculinity forms a part of social change which is running through ourselves, our families, and the institutions of wider society.

(This article was first published in Spanish in the magazine 'Vida y Derecho' (Life and Rights) Number 17 of the FORJA Institute.)

Resources

Understanding Masculinities, M Mac and Ghail (ed), Open University, 1996.
This is the first introductory text to examine the range of different theoretical and methodological approaches to the understanding of masculinity. It brings together overviews of theoretical debates with new empirical material, focusing on different social and cultural areas, and the wide range of masculinities that exist.

Masculinities, R W Connell, Polity Press/ Blackwell, 1995.
Offers a comprehensive introduction to a new field of knowledge and politics. It examines and assesses the history of attempts to understand the nature of masculinity by psychoanalysts, social scientists, and movements for social change. Connell agrees that there is no 'one' masculinity, but multiple masculinities, which can be understood through a social analysis of gender relations. Contemporary developments are examined through a close focus on the lives of four groups of men — some working to transform gender relations, and some resisting such transformations. *Masculinities* then moves to a larger arena, and shows that modern masculinities are products of a 400-year history in which gender was closely connected with empire and the creation of a global economy. The

final section of the book examines new forms of politics about masculinity in Western countries, and discusses how men can pursue social justice.

Theorising Masculinity, H Brod and M Kaufman (eds), Research on Men and Masculinity Series, SAGE Publications, 1994.
Presents ideas borrowed from the disciplines that have fostered the study of masculinities: sociology, psychoanalysis, and ethnography. Explores issues such as power, diversity, ethnicity, feminism, and homophobia. Provides theoretical explanations for militarism, sports, and the men's movement.

Dislocating Masculinities: Comparative Ethnographies, A Cornwall and N Lendisfarne (eds), Routledge, 1994.
Draws upon anthropology, feminism, and post-modernism to provide a challenging study of gender difference. Offers a radical critique of much of the recent writing on men and raises important questions about embodiment, agency, and the relation between masculine style and social contexts.

Contemporary Perspectives on Masculinity: Men, Women and Politics in Modern Society, K Clattebraugh, Westview Press, 1990. Newly updated, 1997.
Surveys the range of responses by men to feminism and puts political theory at the

centre of men's awareness of their own masculinity. Surveys not only conservative, liberal, and radical views of masculinity, but also alternatives offered by the men's movement, spiritual growth activists, and black and gay rights activists. Each of these is explored both as a theoretical perspective and as a social movement.

Boys: Masculinities in Contemporary Culture, P Smith (ed), Westview Press, 1996.
Analysing the meaning of masculinity in contemporary culture, this book examines specific Western cultural male icons (Muhammad Ali, Harvey Kitel, Jean Claude van Damme, Dan Quale, and Newt Gingrich) and critically examines male stereotypes such as the cowboy, the father, the homosexual, and the black terror. Written by cultural studies scholars from departments of film, media studies, English, women's studies, and sociology, the discussion touches on almost every conceivable issue concerning the complex meanings of masculinity in contemporary society.

The Making of Men: Masculinity, Sexuality and Schooling, M Mac an Ghaill, Open University, 1995.
Mac an Ghaill makes a stand as an eloquent, principled, and caring contestant on the side of the oppressed. Includes chapters on schools as a masculinising agency; local student cultures of masculinity; sexuality; learning to become a heterosexual man at school; young women's experiences of teacher and student masculinities; sociology of schooling, equal opportunities and anti-oppression education.

Masculinity in Crisis: Myths, Fantasies and Realities, R Horrocks, MacMillan, 1994.
Argues that masculine identity in Western culture is in deep crisis: old forms of masculinity are disintegrating, while men are struggling to establish new relationships with women and each other. Male identity is shown to be fractured and fragile and truncated. Many stereotypes imprison men — particularly machismo, which is shown to be deeply masochistic and self- destructive.

Language and Masculinity, S Johnson, U H Meinhof, Blackwell, 1997.
This is the first extensive account of male language in the construction of masculinity. Feminist linguistics has come of age. Yet, in more than two decades of research, male speaking-patterns have been largely taken for granted. *Language and Masculinity* asks several important questions. What have we learned specifically about men's language and masculinity? Is it right to assume that men's use of language is the mirror image of what have been considered typically female patterns of interaction? And in what ways does the study of language and masculinities throw new light on assumptions about language and gender?

The Making of Anti-Sexist Men, H Christian, Routledge, 1994.
Do anti-sexist men really exist? If so, who are they and what sort of life experiences produced them? Based around eight interviews with eight men who have responded positively to feminism, this book provides a full discussion of anti-sexist male attitudes.

Male Myths and Icons: Masculinity in Popular Culture, R Horrocks, MacMillan, 1995.
Surveys some of the important myths of masculinity in popular culture, including the western, the horror film, rock music, and pornography. The book argues that popular culture does not simply present tales of male heroism and conquest, but also gives highly complex and ambivalent images of men. The hero turns into anti-hero; feminine and homoerotic material leak in; the male is often shown as the victim. Popular culture, while expressing male hegemony, also reveals images of male defeat, damage and confusion.

Fatherhood Reclaimed: The Making of the Modern Father, A Burges, Vermillion, 1997.
What are the roles of the modern father? How do fathers affect their children? Are good fathers born or made? Do mothers try and shut fathers out? This book challenges assumptions about men as fathers, revealing that parenting behaviour is shaped less by biology than by social conditioning. Men's fathering instincts, strong and innate, are often sabotaged by cultural and social expectations. Draws on diaries — ancient and modern — as well as on research and interviews with fathers from all social groups, to describe what it has meant and means now to be a father.

Family Man: Fatherhood, Housework and Gender Equity, S Coltrane, Oxford University Press, 1996.
According to Scott Coltrane, two-job families are now the rule in America, and fathers are much more involved in raising children, and in housework. Reactions to these changes range from grave misgivings to a sense of liberation and new possibility. *Family Man* explodes many common myths about shared parenting, proves first-hand accounts of men's and women's feelings in two-job families, and reveal some innovative solutions to the problem of balancing job, family, and other commitments.

The Modernization of Fatherhood: a Social and Political History, R LaRossa, University of Chicago, 1997.
Documents shifts in social constructions of fatherhood, both as an institution and as an individual reality. LaRossa's historical analysis of yesterday's fathers shows the unevenness of social change, and provides a means of understanding the continuing diversity of fathers and families.

Fatherhood: Contemporary Theory, Research, and Social Policy, W Marsiglio (ed), from the Research on Men and Masculinities series, SAGE Publications, 1995.
Shifting marriage and divorce patterns, transformation in the workplace, the growth of the women's movement, and development of the men's movement. All these social and cultural changes have changed traditional family roles and forced a re-examination of how fathers and children interact. *Fatherhood* is a collection of theoretical and empirical research on fathers and families. Essays by scholars such as Furstenburg, Seltzer, and Greif, examine differences in culture, class, nationality, and custodial status.

Men, Masculinity and Social Welfare, K Pringle, UCL Press, 1995.
The first full-length study of men and masculinity in relation to social welfare. Considers the issues of the provision and use of welfare services by men, and provides a framework for understanding ways in which men can alter oppressive power relations in welfare agencies and wider society.

Male Responsibility in Today's Africa, Population Reference Bureau, 1996.
Transcript of a radio programme in which four professional men from Kenya, Malawi, Mauritania, and Nigeria discussg the changing role of men in their countries. Sheds special insight on male attitudes towards women and family planning.

'Reputation and respectability reconsidered: a new perspective on Afro-Caribbean peasant women', Besson, J, in *Land and Development in the Caribbean*, J Besson and J Momsen (eds) Macmillan, 1993.
This is a long-overdue re-appraisal of Wilson's landmark construction of Caribbean masculine identity (see below) that criticises it within the context of contemporary gender studies.

The Barbadian male: sexual attitudes and practices G Dann, Macmillan, 1987.
A locally-produced sociological survey of 'Bajan' masculine identity, revealing as much about local analytical construction, as about the people themselves.

The power of sentiment: love, hierarchy, and the Jamaican family elite, L Douglass, Oxford: Westview Press, 1992.
An examination of how notions of sex and power (largely masculine-based) filter through a very hierarchical society, based on fieldwork from within the national 'elite'.

'An evaluation of the 'creolisation' of Trinidad East Indian adolescent masculinity', N M Sampath, in *Trinidad ethnicity*, K A Yelvington, (ed.) London: Macmillan, 1993
Seeks to include Trinidad's Indo-Caribbean community within the discourse of masculine identity, while simultaneously 'de-homogenizing' the predominantly African/Indian discourses of previous Caribbean ethnographies.

Men and Their Families: Contributions of Caribbean Men to Family Life, Caribbean Child Development Centre, Jamaica, 1995.
A handbook for use in schools, churches, and community settings to stimulate discussions of issues such as the roles Caribbean men play in child socialisation and cultural transformation; how these roles and the roles women play can be strengthened, harnessed, and consciously changed; to remind men and women of the importance of their beliefs and behaviour patterns; and to extend and enrich through the recording of group experiences the collective knowledge and literature about Caribbean families and family life. Includes guidelines for discussions of male family roles, and step-by-step instructions that facilitators can use while planning workshops.

What's He doing at the Family Centre? The Dilemmas of Men Who Care for Children, S Ruxton, National Children's Home Action for Children, 1993.
Explores why so few men work in family centres, and the dilemmas of those who do.

Identifies the influences and constraints which affect the way in which male workers interact with children and their parents, and with other staff. Data was initially gathered through a questionnaire sent to male and female staff in 77 family centres run by the National Children's Home.

White Guys: Studies in Postmodern Domination and Difference, F Pfeil, Verso, 1995
Expose contradictions in the construction of white heterosexual masculinity in American popular culture. Probes such topics as the rock'n'roll bodies of Bruce Springsteen, Axl Rose, and the late Kurt Cobain; the 'male rampage' films *Die Hard and Lethal Weapon* and films of 'sensitive transformation'; and the curious yet symptomatic activities of the men's movement whose 'rituals' Pfeil has investigated first-hand.

My Life as a Male Anorexic, Michael Krasnow, The Haworth Press, USA, 1995.
The autobiographical account of a young man's ongoing struggle with anorexia. Sheds light on the little-known or discussed problem of male anorexia.

Articles and papers

'Status of Women; Status of Men: Perspectives on Masculinity, Gender and Development with reference to Bangladesh', Paper for Edinburgh Conference on Boundaries and Identities, S C White, University of East Anglia.
Argues that the failure of Gender and Development literature to attend to the gender dimension of male identity seriously inhibits our understanding of gender relations by leaving men vulnerable to stereotyping as patriarchal figures. The study of masculinity can contribute significant questions to the dominant models of gender analysis, particularly those used within the gender and development context.

'Technology and Masculinity: The Case of the Computer', M Lie, *The European Journal of Women's Studies* 2, 1995
Asks why women become 'invisible' when working with technology. Suggests that it may be because technology is so closely connected to men and masculinity that activities within this field are categorised as something else when they appear in the heads and hands of women. Argues that in order to understand women's relationship to technology we also have to study men and masculinity.

'Men at Work', M Hequet, *Training Magazine*, January, 1995
Report on a men's 'efficacy seminar', designed to 'foster collaboration in today's diverse workplace, and to acknowledge the unprecedented turmoil' men are experiencing in their work and family lives.' The seminar included lectures on how men grow up, and on men's relationships with their parents and peers at work. It emphasised communication and relationship building, 'because that's where men need the most help.'

'Men, Masculinity and Feminism', W Cloete, *Siren News* 3: 1, 1995.
Argues that the central problem about masculinity, is that it did not exist until feminist attacks on the political and social theory that assure men and their masculinity a privileged social position; the gay rights movement also placed masculinity in the spot light. Explores issues around the relationships between gay men, feminism and gender identity.

'Modern Swedish Fatherhood:
The Challenges and the Opportunities', G Swedin, *Reproductive Health Matters* 7, 1996.
Discusses the consequences of changing Swedish views about fatherhood, and shares some experiences of fathers' training groups, and the ways in which men's parenting skills are growing and bringing them closer to their children.

'Flirting in the Factory', K A Yelvington, *Journal of the Royal Anthropological Institute* (N.S.) 2 , 1996; 313—333
As a participant-observer within an urban Trinidadian electrical-goods factory, Yelvington analyses notions of erotic identity along the axes of ethnicity, class, and gender.

'Reputation and respectability:
a suggestion for Caribbean ethnography', P J Wilson, *Man* (N.S.) 4, 1969 70—84.
P J Wilson *Crab antics*, New Haven: Yale University Press, 1973.
Wilson's benchmark notions of masculine reputation/respectability created the analytical paradigm around which all other Caribbean analytical ethnographies revolve, whether in agreement or not.

'Space for a Man: The Transformation of Masculinity in 20th Century Culture', J Frykman, *Reproductive Health Matters* 7, 1996.
Looks at how current struggles to define a male identity, based in the home, lead to highly diverse definitions of what is typically masculine. It uses Sweden not just as an example of equality, but also as an illustration of how plastic and complex masculinity actually is.

'I'll Show You Mine If You'll Show Me Yours', G W Dowsett, *Reproductive Health Matters* 7, 1996.
Describes the growing gap between gay and non-gay men and women, with regard to relations with women, differences to feminist thinking, concerns of daily life, dealing with the HIV/AIDS epidemic and sex. Challenges feminists and heterosexual men to address the issues of homosexuality and homophobia as an integral part of understanding masculine heterosexual sex, masculinity and sexual politics.

'Men's Needs and Responsibilities', special issue on *Planned Parenthood Challenges*, 1996/2
Articles challenge the popular image of

man being the initiator in sexuality and being in control of it. Suggests that both men and women suffer from the discrepancy between the superman myth and the reality. Articles include: masculinity and the male role in sexual health; finding the right sexual health services for young men; Arab World male programmes; and converting Bangladesh's influential religious leaders.

'Men in the Lives of Children',
special issue of *Coordinators' Notebook:
An International Resources for Early
Childhood Development* 16, 1995.
Includes articles on men and their children, and gender relations and conflicts in fathering in Africa, Asia and Europe.

Magazines, newsletters and journals

Men in Families; Hombres en Familias
Publishes information about fathering research and intervention programs with the aim of sharing information and expertise in the Americas. Published in both Spanish and English.
Patrice Engle, Ph.D. California Polytech Institute, San Luis Obispo, CA 93407 USA.

Journal of Men's Studies
Male feminist magazine available from the Men's Studies Press. PO Box 32, Harriman TN 37748-0032, USA

Working with Men
This quarterly newsletter looks at issues related to masculinity and sexism, in health, education, probation, careers, social work, youth work, community work and other professions. Focuses on practice and related issuese. Working with Men, c/o 320 commercial Way, London, SE15 1QN, UK. Tel: 44 0171 732 9409

Achilles Heel
Biannual publication that acts as a forum for discussion of men and masculinity. Achilles Heel, 10 Ashbourne Grove, London, SE22 8RL, England.

M.E.N. Magazine
Its mission is to provide information, support and advocacy for men. Articles have focused on men and grief, domestic violence, gender and reconciliation, love and betrayal, and reports on men's national conferences. M.E.N. Magazine Editorial Office, 7552 31st Ave, N.E. Seattle, WA 98115
For a sample issue, send e-mail to menmag@wln.com

NGOs, organisations and groups

Men for Non-Violence (NZ) Inc
National umbrella group for organisations throughout New Zealand which work with violent men in their communities helping them to change their abusive behaviour. Men for Non-violence (NZ) Inc, Box 10 632, The Tefrace, Wellington, New Zealand. Tel: (04) 499 6384. Fax: (04) 499 6387.

Men for Change
A pro-feminist organisation for men, dedicated to working with women to promote gender equity and end sexism and violence.
http:/www.cfn.cs.dal.ca/CommunitySupport/Men4Change/
m4c_back.html

American Men's Studies Association
An organisation dedicated to teaching, research, and clinical practice in the field of men's studies. Its objectives are to encourage the refinement of the parameters of men's studies, to generate theory and to develop methodologies of the study of masculinity from a perspective that eschews

oppression in all forms. AMSA Membership Office, 329 Afton Ave, Youngstown, Ohio, USA 44512-2311. Tel: (1) 216 782 2730

Father to Father

A national American effort to unite men in the task of being a strong and positive force in their children's lives. Plans to expand and enhance existing father support programmes, create new opportunities for men to come together in their role as fathers. Martha Erickson, Univ of Minnesota, 1985 Buford Ave, St Paul, MN 55108 Tel: (1) 612 622 1212 http://www.cyfc.umn.edu/Fathernet/ftf.html

Real Men

An anti-sexist men's organisation dedicated to eliminating sexism, misogyny and male violence. Contrary to the popular stereotype about 'real men' as macho tough guy, it is important for men to rethink and work to change traditional masculinity. Real Men, P.O.Box 1769 Brookline, MA 02146, USA. Tel: (1) 617 782 7838

Men Against Domestic Violence

A coalition of men working to address the issue of domestic violence against women. Babtunde Folayemi, 814 Laguna St., Santa Barbara, Ca. 93101

International Planned Parenthood Foundation

Has published reports on men's support of family planning and their need for more effective contraception; sex education from a male perspective; male hormonal contraception; and on the male-friendly approach to family planning in Africa. Regent's College, Inner Circle, Regent's Park, London, NW1 4NS, UK
Tel: (44) (0)171 487 0741
Fax: (44) (0)171 487 7950
E-mail: jgizbert@ippf.attmail.com

Population Reference Bureau, Inc
1875 Connecticut Ave NW, Suite 520, Washington DC 20009
Tel: (202) 483-1100

Internet resources

Full-Time Dads — The Online Magazine

Supports and encourages men as fathers. 'Through open exchanges of ideas, we can end the isolation and become better fathers.' Includes reviews of books on parenting, kids, fatherhood, and articles on issues such as homeschooling. http://www.parentsplace.com/readroom/fulltdad/index.html

FatherNet

Information on the importance of fathering and how fathers can be good parents and parent educators. Includes research, policy, and opinion documents about the factors that support or hinder men's involvement in the lives of children. Includes research papers on young unwed fathers and welfare reform encouraging responsible fatherhood. http://www.cyfc.umn.edu/fathernet/index.html

Fathering Magazine

An online magazine that includes articles on the joy of fathering, the importance of fathers, fathering fiction, fathering advice and fathering in the 1990s. http://www.fathermag.com/

Working for Justice... Ending Violence

A website for profeminist activists. Provides a forum for activists working to end violence and oppression, in particular, profeminist men's activism to end violence against women and children. http://www.geocities.com/CapitolHill/5863/

PROFEM mail list

An internet mail list that focuses on men, masculinities and gender relations — promote dialogue and networking among men and women concerned with gender justice and the elimination of sexism. Supports men's efforts towards positive personal and social change. Circulates information on new initiatives, research

and resources. To subscribe, send an e-mail message with "subscribe profem-1" to: majordomo@coombs.edu.au
To unsubscribe, send the message "unsubscribe profem-1 to
 majordomo@coombs.edu.au

MensNet

Canadian coast-to-coast, pro-feminist, gay affirmative, anti-racist, male positive network. Includes articles on topics relating to men, gender, politics, pro-feminism, progressive social change and spirituality.
http://infoweb.magi.com/^mensnet/

XY Magazine

An Australian nonprofit internet magazine about men and masculinity. A space for the exploration of issues of gender and sexuality, and practical discussions of the hows and whys of personal change. XY is male positive, pro-feminist and pro-gay.
http://www.coombs.anu.edu.ac/^gorkin/xy/xyf.htm